THE REPUBLIC OF LEBANON

PROFILES • NATIONS OF THE CONTEMPORARY MIDDLE EAST
Bernard Reich and David E. Long, Series Editors

The Republic of Lebanon: Nation in Jeopardy, David C. Gordon
Jordan: Crossroads of Middle Eastern Events, Peter Gubser
South Yemen: A Marxist Republic in Arabia, Robert W. Stookey
Syria: Modern State in an Ancient Land, John Devlin
Turkey, George S. Harris
Iraq, Phebe Marr
Sudan, John Voll and Sarah Voll
United Arab Emirates, Malcolm Peck
North Yemen, Manfred W. Wenner

Also of Interest

The New Arab Social Order: A Study of the Social Impact of Oil Wealth, Saad Eddin Ibrahim
OPEC: Twenty Years and Beyond, edited by Ragaei W. El Mallakh
Economic Growth and Development in Jordan, Michael P. Mazur
The United Arab Emirates: Unity in Fragmentation, Ali Mohammed Khalifa
Libya: The Experience of Oil, J. A. Allan
Food, Development, and Politics in the Middle East, Marvin G. Weinbaum

THE
REPUBLIC OF
LEBANON
Nation in Jeopardy

David C. Gordon

Westview Press • Boulder, Colorado

Croom Helm • London and Canberra

Profiles/Nations of the Contemporary Middle East

Jacket photos (*clockwise from upper left*): Palestinian guerrilla; produce arrives on the outskirts of Beirut; reconstructing Beirut in the early 1980s; Palestinian refugees, 1980. Credits: 1 and 4—Mark Lane; 2 and 3—*Middle East Insight*.

Published in 1983 in the United States of America by
  Westview Press, Inc.
  5500 Central Avenue
  Boulder, Colorado 80301
  Frederick A. Praeger, President and Publisher

Published in 1983 in Great Britain by
  Croom Helm Ltd.
  Provident House, Burrell Row,
  Beckenham, Kent, BR3 1AT

Library of Congress Catalog Card Number 82-20108
ISBN (U.S.) 0-86531-450-0
ISBN (U.K.) 0-7099-1154-8

Printed and bound in the United States of America

10 9 8 7 6 5 4 3

FOR DAVID DODGE

A mortal splendor: meteors are not needed
less than mountains: shine, perishing
republic.

Robinson Jeffers

Contents

Tables and Illustrations

Tables

Illustrations

Preface

In this study of the Lebanese Republic the approach is topical rather than historical, although it draws upon the historical record for examples and parallels. The subject is Lebanon since independence in 1943 through its agony since 1975. The reader at whom this book is aimed is versed in international affairs but has no particular expertise regarding Lebanon.

Because statistics for Lebanon are often impressionistic—no official census, for example, has been taken since 1932, and chaotic conditions since 1975 preclude the gathering of reliable data in many cases—figures employed in this book will sometimes be for years and time spans that may seem remote in time. Such figures are often more reliable than those for later years as indications of conditions and trends. Thus, for example, fairly reliable data for the years immediately after 1958 were provided by an extensive study of the Lebanese society and economy under President Shihab, a study not since repeated. In addition to the unreliability of much statistical data, a study of a nation in civil war and serving as an arena for international conflict is beset by several other difficulties. Among them is the problem of nomenclature—some conservatives, for example, refuse to consider the conflict since 1975 as a "civil war," Prime Minister Begin has denied that Israeli actions in June 1982 constituted an "invasion," and some radicals do not consider Lebanon to have ever been a legitimate "nation." Every attempt will be made in what follows to use neutral terms or to use charged terms neutrally.

Another difficulty in the present undertaking is to decide in many cases what time frame to use; several institutions, for example, may already be moribund or may disappear in the near future, while still treated as in existence in descriptive contexts. The writer has sometimes felt he has been writing on water and begs the reader's understanding.

xi

As for the problem of possible bias, of feeling, for example, closer to either the position of the Palestinians or that of the Lebanese nationalists, the writer can only hope that he has been objective and has stuck to the thin line between sympathy and empathy.

Perhaps the greatest difficulty the author has confronted has been to make some sense for the reader of the terrible complexity of the Lebanese experience without oversimplification. Whether he has succeeded or not is for the reader to judge. But it might be useful to provide, for the neophyte in particular, a simplified preview of what is to follow.

In the introductory chapter natural and human geographical factors are discussed, and the great variety of religious sects that make up Lebanon are described. Roughly half the Lebanese belong to Christian sects, half to Muslim sects. It will be seen how various and how mutually incompatible are many sectarian attitudes, points of view, and ideologies, making it very difficult to sustain a community that can survive only on compromise and mutual accommodation. The basic rift running through the national experience has been mainly (but not exclusively) between Christians who favor a Western orientation for the country and who fear Arab nationalism, and Muslims who favor an Eastern and pro-Arab orientation. Fortunately for the survival of Lebanon, substantial numbers of Christians and Muslims have been willing to compromise, especially in times of prosperity and reduced tension in the area. In times of tension and crisis, however, compromise has proved difficult.

In Chapter 2 a historical survey of Lebanon is provided, arranged thematically rather than chronologically. Running through this history is the thread of mutual coexistence alternating with periods of dissension between the sects, usually culminating in the imposition of a new political arrangement by outside powers, until Lebanon finally became independent in 1943. Once independent, Lebanon was able to fend for itself on the basis of the so-called National Pact, by which Christian leaders agreed not to steer the nation too far toward the West and Muslim leaders agreed not to steer it too far toward the East. Lebanon survived its first major challenge with the civil strife of 1958, however precariously, but succumbed in the disaster of the Civil War from 1975 to this day.

Chapter 3 deals with Lebanese society, a prosperous and rapidly "modernizing" one that yet retains traditional mores and ways. Unique among Arab nations, Lebanon remained until 1975 a liberal, free-enterprise society, as well as an important cultural center and a crossroads between the Western and Eastern worlds. The tensions and rifts already mentioned, however, continued to dominate the culture and the educational system and, in turn, to be reinforced by these.

In Chapter 4 the economy of Lebanon is discussed, an economy that has thrived because of the mercantile talents of the Lebanese yet has been vulnerable because of its heavy dependence on services and invisible sources of income and because of the great disparities in income among classes, sects, and regions. Efforts after 1958 to provide for greater social justice and to confront disparities were made, but on the whole these were largely ineffective. Since 1975 the economy has been in disarray, but paradoxically, many individual Lebanese thrive and the private sector, although not the public sector, prospers in many spheres. For many Lebanese, however, conditions are dismal indeed.

Chapter 5 deals with the political system of Lebanon, a system that has been democratic and parliamentary but based upon the distribution of power and authority along sectarian lines. Although political participation is granted to all sects, the Christian Maronites have in general been at the top of the heap, the Muslim Shi'ites at the bottom. In calm times the system provides for stability, but also for immobility. In critical times, when hard decisions have to be made, stability tends to give way to instability and even to violence, and this system, which relies on compromise and so tends to be immobilist, can be threatened with collapse. One important factor discussed is the overflow of the Arab-Israeli conflict—a conflict the Lebanese can do little about—across the Lebanese borders. The presence of the Palestinians (400,000 in 1981) has been fateful; for them Lebanon has become a base for attacks upon Israel, as well as a refuge, and their presence has exposed Lebanon to reprisal raids and even invasions by Israel. The Palestinian presence came to be seen by many Lebanese, particularly the Christians, as a threat to their sovereignty and by radical leftist Lebanese, as well as many Muslims, as an ally in their efforts to change or revolutionize the nation. The Palestinian presence, it will be seen, was one factor that further split the Lebanese and constituted one cause for the Civil War.

In Chapter 6, the Civil War is analyzed, its costs estimated, and the possibility of its leading to the destruction of Lebanon considered. In Chapter 7, Lebanon between 1976 and 1982 is characterized as a patchwork of power centers—Syrian, Palestinian, rightist Christian, and others—only nominally under the control of the legitimate government. Lebanon continued to be an arena in which the Israelis and Arabs, the Arab states among themselves, and other powers, continued to confront one another at the expense of the Lebanese, but never as brutally as after Israel's invasion on June 6. The consequences of this invasion are considered in Chapter 8.

For the author, who has spent many years in Lebanon and grown to love its people, it has been painful to dwell upon this nation's ordeal. And this has also been true of Ann Gordon, who has helped editorially in the composition of this book, and to whom I am grateful. I would also like to thank Susan McRory of Westview Press for her very able copy editing and Donna Egan, Mark Lane, George Nader of *Middle East Insight,* and Grace Thomas for their kindness in allowing me to use their photographs.

D.C.G.

1

Introduction

After 1975, Lebanon, a coastal Mediterranean nation smaller than the state of Connecticut and populated by some 3 million, was in a state of disarray and, in some regions, disaster. In 1982 its very existence as a nation was in jeopardy. Why bother to consider it in its own right? one might well ask. Why not treat it simply as the battlefield of larger conflict it appeared to be? After all, the Republic of Lebanon was little more than a complex of hostile and armed enclaves, each beholden directly or indirectly to a foreign body. And it had been an independent republic only since 1943, a period of less than four decades. An agglomeration of different ethnic groups, it seemed never to have developed the inner core or established the legitimacy of a nation, as had, for example, Uri, Schwyz, and Unterwalden after 1291 and the United Provinces after 1581, two small coalitions that fought the powerful Hapsburgs to emerge as Switzerland and the Netherlands, respectively. Why bother, indeed, with this apparent historical will-o-the-wisp?

As a rationale for the present undertaking, one might reply with the following brief observations. Although Lebanon as an independent nation is very young, the Lebanese experience in multiethnic coexistence, even if often beset by conflict, has roots deep in the seventeenth century, if under several different umbrellas—Ottoman, Egyptian, and French. It has often proved to be a viable and even a prosperous entity, and until recently, compared to most of its fellow Arab states, it was genuinely liberal, open, and republican, with a relatively high standard of living and endowed with some of the best universities and publishing centers in the Middle East. In addition, it has served international finance and commerce as the hub of regional activities and has been an important center for culture and recreation for Europeans, Americans, and other Arabs alike. Even in disaster its entrepreneurial spirit, echoing the remote Phoenicians, has been impressive and augurs well for the future.

In addition, Lebanon has been a laboratory for ethnologists and other students of multiethnic coexistence—even if only as a negative

1

model—this in a world concerned with coexistence on a global scale, with reconciling and integrating diverse peoples into "legitimate," pluralistic combinations. Perhaps Lebanon may serve only to show what to avoid; more optimistically, it may show that multiethnic coexistence is possible, even with internal flaws, unless destroyed by extrinsic forces. In any case, Lebanon is a small part of the world that needs to be understood, if only as one of the most dangerous points of confrontation on the perilous international scene.

SETTING

Before the twentieth century, the entity called Lebanon consisted (except for occasional periods when under strong princes it held sway over Beirut and the Biqa' [Bekaa] Valley) of the Mountain, a rugged, gorged, and valleyed area reaching at spots to the coast. This Mountain, running north to south, is separated from the eastern Anti-Lebanon range—also running north-south and dividing today's Republic of Syria from Lebanon—by the fertile Biqa' Valley. It is the Anti-Lebanon range, snow-covered in winter, that provides the country's name (probably from "white" in Aramaic) and makes possible the rain and the streams that feed the coast. It was only in 1920, when the French created Greater Lebanon, that the entity came to include the Biqa' Valley, Beirut, Tripoli and environs to the north, and Sidon and environs to the south. Lebanon is bordered by Syria to the north and the east, Israel to the south, and the Mediterranean Sea to the west. The small size of this nation can be gauged by the fact that Beirut is only a three-to-four-hour drive by car from Damascus and that any part of Lebanon can be reached easily within half a day.

Mount Lebanon, which rises to 10,000 feet (3,000 meters) at its highest point, and the Anti-Lebanon, which rises to 9,000 feet (2,700 meters) and continues south to the Hermon range, which is about the same height, embrace the Biqa' Valley, which is 3,000 feet (900 meters) above sea level; it is here that two of Lebanon's important rivers, the Orontes going north and the Litani going south, have their sources. Both the Biqa' and the Anti-Lebanon are drier than the west. In Mount Lebanon springs make it possible to cultivate crops 5,000 feet (1,500 meters) up by the use of terracing; bananas can be grown on the coast; olives, vines, and figs can be cultivated on the low foothills; cereals, apricots, and pears on the middle slopes; and apples and potatoes on the higher levels.

Lebanon is one of the most heavily urbanized parts of the Arab world. By 1975 some 61 percent of the population lived in urban centers of more than 5,000. Among the confessions, 84 percent of the Sunnites,

60 percent of the Greek Orthodox, 45 percent of the Maronites, 55 percent of the Shi'ites, and 55 percent of the Druzes lived in urban areas. Only Bahrain among the Arab states was more densely populated than Lebanon: Lebanon's population density was 1,295 persons per square mile (498 per square kilometer).

Although the climate, generally, is moderate Mediterranean, there are different zones, each with its own particular characteristics; the coast is humid in summer, cold in winter; the high mountains are very cold and snow-covered during much of the period from September to April and refreshingly cool in summer; and the Biqa' has low humidity in summer and is cold and has strong winds in winter. Skiing is available in winter in the mountains; swimming, most of the year. Once an important silk producer, Lebanon now produces mainly fruits, vegetables, wine, and tobacco, like other Mediterranean lands, and like each of these, it has—or had at one time—its own particular charm, both as a resort and as a place to live and work. And like these it is rich in relics and monuments of many centuries of history. In Lebanon, in particular, this past is easily accessible as well as abundant.

As impressive as any monument is the grove of the famous Cedars of Bsharrah, which recalls biblical times and serves as a national symbol. In Beirut, the Grand Mosque of 'Umar, its base stones Roman and Byzantine, was a Crusader cathedral until its conversion in the thirteenth century. Rome is everywhere; in the aqueduct outside Beirut, in small temples, mosaics, and the monumental remains of Baalbeck. Relics of the Phoenicians can be found in Byblos, around the well-preserved Crusader castle, and in Tyre, where a Roman hippodrome has also been uncovered. The Mamluks of the fourteenth century are represented by several watchtowers along the coast, the Ayyubids by the extant castle of Mousayliha, the Umayyads of the eighth century by the castle-resort of Anjar, the amirate of Bashir II by the beautifully decorated nineteenth-century palace of Beit ad-Din, and the Crusaders by several castles besides Byblos, including one on Sidon's shore and Beaufort, which looks into Israel and had until June 1982 withstood heavy and frequent bombardment. At the mouth of the Dog River (Nahr al-Kalb) plaques commemorate the passage of the Assyrians (seventh century B.C.), the Romans (third century A.D.), and Napoleon III (1860), among others. A more recent plaque commemorates the departure of the last French troops on December 31, 1946. Myth pervades the countryside. A structure at Nebi Yunis is claimed to be the tomb of Noah; a small chapel-mosque (al-Khadr) where St. George killed the dragon; and the Nahr Ibrahim in March and April is said to flow with the blood of Adonis (the color results from minerals in the riverbed).

MULTIETHNICITY

The most important fact about Lebanon's human geography is the multiplicity of sectarian or confessional communities, Christian, Muslim, and other, not one of which can claim to constitute a majority. The Lebanese entity was predominantly Christian before the creation of Greater Lebanon in 1920, but since then Muslims have had the edge numerically and today the Muslim Shi'ites probably constitute the largest sect. Fertility rates have been generally higher among Muslims than among Christians, even though Islam allows for contraception and Catholicism does not. And the creation of Greater Lebanon, by bringing into the entity areas that were predominantly Muslim, had obvious important social and political consequences. Officially, the census of 1932 has remained the basis for the distribution of public and political power and authority; proposals to take a new census have been considered a threat by many Christians. Acceptance of the 1932 census, which showed Christians to be a majority, has thus been one of the compromises that has made the nation a possibility. Officially, the largest confession remains the Maronite, and the largest Muslim confession, the Sunnite.

Another important demographic factor is that while in certain districts one sect or another may predominate, in all areas there is overlapping, even within particular villages—a reality that makes both for unity and, in troubled times, for a dangerous struggle for turf. Each confession has its own sense of community, but none is monolithic. Within each there are extended-family rivalries and competing interests, and although communities tend to be exclusive and self-enclosed in some ways, they have also been interwoven in a common destiny, and on some levels of social and political discourse, they interact and cooperate with one another. It is this cooperation that affords Lebanon the chance of becoming a viable nation. Even if the threat of disintegration and warfare has always been present, and even if the appellation the "Switzerland of the East" now sounds stale and hollow, there have been periods when the nation has flourished with a common and communal ethos.

At the end of the sixteenth century the larger part of the Mountain was occupied by Shi'ites, while the Maronites were grouped in the north and the Druzes in the south, particularly in the Shuf (the region south of Beirut). During the seventeenth and eighteenth centuries the Maronites expanded south and the Druzes north; the Shi'ites lost much of their land. As the Maronites moved south into Kisrwan, they rebelled against Shi'ite overlords and drove the Shi'ites out; in general the Shi'ites were forced out of the central part of the Mountain to occupy the periphery, as they do today. The Maronites penetrated the Druze Shuf to become agricultural workers under Dru: lords. The alliance of Maronite and Druze was dominant. The mass of the Sunnites, and many Greek Orthodox, entered the system only with the creation of Greater Lebanon in 1920, when Beirut and the littoral were integrated finally, as they had previously been occasionally, into the Lebanese entity.

Among the important Christian groups are Uniate Catholics— Catholics who are under the pope's authority but practice particular rites of their own. These groups include Maronites, Greek Catholics, and Armenian Catholics. Other Christian groups include Roman Catholics, Armenian (Gregorian) Orthodox, Greek Orthodox, and Nestorian Assyrians. Muslim groups include the Shi'ites (called Mitawalis in Lebanon) and Sunnites. The Druzes, although they are often grouped with Muslims, have a faith of their own. In all, the number of sects is twenty-two. Each of these forms one or another of the tesserae of what is sometimes called the Lebanese mosaic; the dynamic by which each acts as a unit and interacts with the others is usually termed "confessionalism" or "sectarianism" (ta'ifiya in Arabic).

The Maronites took their name from the fourth-century pious monk Marun. Led by Patriarch Yuhanna Marun (died c. 707), they sought sanctuary in the Qadishah Valley of Lebanon in the seventh century after troubles with the Byzantine government and with Jacobites (a Syrian sect holding that Christ has only one nature) in western Syria. Eventually, in 1790, Bkirke was made the headquarters of the Maronite patriarchs "of Antioch and the Rest of the Orient." Originally monothelite (that is, holding that Christ has one will but two natures), they entered into partial communion with Rome in the twelfth century and into full communion in 1736. The patriarch is elected by a conclave of Maronite bishops; if no choice can be made within fifteen days, the pope in Rome makes the appointment. Maronites in the main have aligned themselves over the centuries with the West—with the Crusaders, for example, and with Napoleon during the siege of Acre (1799)—and they maintain close cultural and emotional ties to France. Constantin-François Volney, the famous eighteenth-century traveler, remarked on their independent-mindedness, but he also warned, prophetically, of their religious passion and rigidity. The Maronites constituted the bulk of the inhabitants of the Mountain proper and continue to be the plurality there to this day.

The Greek Catholics (also called Melchites) are the descendants of a group of Greek Orthodox who in 1724 left that church and, while keeping their Greek rites, entered into communion with Rome. Their

Roman ruins, Baalbeck. (Credit: Mark Lane)

Roman ruins, Baalbeck. (Credit: Mark Lane)

Beaufort Castle, a strategic height captured by Israel in 1982. (Credit: Ellen Harris, *Middle East Insight*)

religious leader is the patriarch of Antioch, Alexandria, Jerusalem, and the rest of the Orient, traditionally resident in Cairo. Their chief city in Lebanon is Zahlah, at the foot of Mount Sannin. The patriarchs of the other Uniate groups, the Syrian Catholics and the Armenian Catholics, reside in Beirut. The Armenian Catholics, as well as the Armenian Orthodox, have the Armenian language as bearer of their particular non-Arab heritage. Both arrived in Lebanon in large numbers after the Armenian massacres at the hands of the Turks before, during, and after World War I. The leading patriarch of the Armenian Orthodox is the catholicos of Etchmiadzin in Soviet Armenia.

Those Greek Orthodox who are Arab by identity (in contrast to Greeks, Russians, and others) come under a patriarch who resides in Damascus or under one who resides in Cairo. Unlike the Maronites, who are concentrated in Lebanon, the Greek Orthodox are widely dispersed in different parts of historical Syria, that is, the area including the modern states of Jordan, Israel, Lebanon, and Syria.

The Nestorian Assyrians are a distinct people who sought refuge in Lebanon after the 1933 massacre of their people in Iraq. Other smaller groups residing in Lebanon are Protestants, Roman Catholics, and non-

TABLE 1.1   Confessional Distribution

| | Mountain | | Lebanon | | Beirut |
	1865	1932	1956	1977	1956
Maronites	172,000	226,378	424,000	23%	18,000
Druzes	29,000	53,047	88,000	7%	--
Greek Orthodox	30,000	76,522	149,000	7%	25,000
Greek Catholics	19,000	45,999	91,000	5%	4,000
Sunnites	8,000	175,925	286,000	26%	76,000
Shi'ites	10,000	154,208	250,000	27%	17,000
Armenians		31,156	79,000	--	--
Others (including Jews, Protestants, Syrian Orthodox, Latins, Nestorian Chaldeans)			44,000		
Total:	266,661	785,543	1,411,000		

Largest Concentrations (1956 approximate)

Maronites	Mountain:	225,000; north:	112,000
Greek Orthodox	north:	63,000	
Greek Catholics	south:	23,000; Biqa':	36,000
Sunnites	north:	118,000	
Shi'ites	south:	149,000	

Source: Adapted from Michael Hudson, The Precarious Republic: Modernization in Lebanon (New York: Random House, 1968), pp. 22, 58.

Christian minorities, including Baha'is and Jews, of whom there were about 6,000 in 1975.

Among the Muslims are the Shi'ites, members of a branch of Islam that traces the line of descent of the caliphate (succession to the Prophet) from 'Ali, nephew and son-in-law of Muhammad, through the twelfth *imam* in succession, who is held to have disappeared for a time, to return one day as *mahdi*, or messianic savior. The Sunnites, who accept the historical line of succession as valid, are members of the mainstream of Islam in most Arab Muslim countries; since the fourteenth century, they have been the dominant Muslim group in the area. The Kurds are Sunnites, but they speak their own language and have their own identity and historical memory.

Finally, the Druzes, whose leading family, the Ma'ns, laid the foundations of Lebanon in the seventeenth century from their center in the Shuf, were originally Muslims who developed their own identity in the eleventh century when they were converted to the teachings of the Isma'ili Shi'ite Fatimid caliph, al-Hakim (died 1021). The details of their syncretistic and theosophic faith are kept secret by the *'uqqal*, the initiated learned ones. They practice *taqiyya* (pious dissimulation) when necessary, reject converts, marry among themselves, believe in metempsychosis, and prefer to be known as *Muwahiddun* (unitarians). In 1975, there were 400,000 to 450,000 Druzes, 150,000 to 170,000 of whom lived in Lebanon; the rest lived in Syria and Israel. Charles Churchill, who witnessed the massacre by the Druzes of many Maronites in 1860, described the fierce bellicosity of the Druzes when aroused and their communal pride and cohesion.

In 1948, with the creation of Israel, about 200,000 Palestinian refugees arrived in Lebanon. The bulk were Sunnites, but many were Christians. Unlike the Armenians, they have not been granted citizenship en masse, nor, as a self-conscious ethnic group bent upon return to their homes, have most wanted to become Lebanese. After the 1967 Arab-Israeli war and the 1970 military defeat of the Palestinians in Jordan, the number of Palestinians in Lebanon rose to 400,000 to 500,000.

IDENTIFICATION

Except for the Armenians and Kurds, the mother tongue of the Lebanese is Arabic, and Arabic is the language of social intercourse in general. However, because the private sector of education is often foreign and continues to emphasize foreign languages (French and English in particular) and because Lebanon has been a merchant-republic, bilingualism and trilingualism are widespread, in some cases to the detriment of the Arabic language itself. Language has symbolic significance as a dimension of identification; for example, there are Christian families that use French more regularly than they do Arabic. Some extremist Lebanese nationalists, particularly among the Maronites, would go so far as to make the colloquial Lebanese Arabic dialect the language of education in place of classical Arabic, which is the sacred language of Islam, a common heritage of all educated Arabs, and the most important basis for Arab nationalism (an ideology many if not most Maronites condemn). The use of the Lebanese dialect would serve to further separate Lebanon from the rest of the Arab world and so strengthen Lebanon's particularity. For the Armenians, who learn Arabic for business purposes, their language is the symbol of their non-Arab identity. They tend to live unto themselves and have their own political parties—the progressive Tashnaq, the centrist Ramgavar, and the Marxist social-democratic Hentchaq, which has affiliations with Soviet Armenia. Both they and the Kurds dream of someday having states of their own. They have, nevertheless, been on the whole a creative and industrious element in Lebanon and have shown their gratitude for the haven they have received.

Language, dress, mosques and churches, accents, and other signs and symbols distinguish one sect from another, adding to the extraordinary variegation of this small land. Names such as Michel and Pierre are tips that a person is Christian, Ahmad and Muhammad that he is Muslim—while Suleiman, Sarah, and Ibrahim can be either, indicating the common sources of Islam and Christianity.

This proliferation of identities, while constituting a source of fascinating variety and cultural wealth, also, unfortunately, serves to reinforce differences and has been a barrier to social integration. It is not strange that Lebanon has been described as "improbable," "fragmented," and "precarious," as a "mosaic" that has never attained to genuine pluralism, or realized a consensus or a true national legitimacy. To most Lebanese, identification has been confessional, and partly for confessional reasons, loyalties have often been to extra-Lebanese ideologies—Pan-Arabism, for example, or Greater Syrianism. And even when the loyalty of a community such as the Maronites has been to Lebanon, it has often been expressed in so sectarian and exclusive a manner that it has only antagonized the other confessions, confirming them in their own identifications. In troubled times, the singing of the national anthem or waving of the flag has been perceived by some as provocative and reactionary. Conversely, extra-Lebanese symbols—such as the picture of the modern Egyptian Saladin, Gamal Abdel Nasser (Jamal 'Abd al-Nasir), who in the 1950s and 1960s threatened to sweep the Arab world into unity, or the flag of the United Arab Republic (UAR), representing the temporary (1958–1961) unification of Syria and Egypt, a step in this direction—have been perceived by some as threatening and treasonable. In such times of tension, symbols invite countersymbols, and normally muted expressions of identification become vocal, even bellicose.

In tranquil times, cement to hold the mosaic in place has come from mutual interest (prosperity in business, for example), hostility to a common outsider (the Ottoman Turks, for example, on the eve of World War I, and the French, during World War II), and the exercise of courtesy and toleration (even if these are often motivated by pragmatism). But in abnormal times—1860, 1958, and 1975, for example—buried sentiments of hostility emerge and communal identification becomes more pronounced and more explicit.

These identifications, long in the making, are rooted in historical memory—the Crusades are still symbolically important in Lebanon among both Christians and Muslims, and the massacres of Maronites in 1860 are still recalled on a mass level. These identifications are, of course, rooted in religious faith and, even where agnosticism prevails, in the customs and the practices of the confession.

In the context of independent Lebanon, identifications might be seen to fall along a spectrum marked at one extreme by a fierce loyalty to a Lebanon seen as totally sovereign, as having a non-Arab identity, and as tied by culture and orientation to the Christian West, France in particular. At the other extreme is the conviction that Lebanon, even if independent, is an essential and inevitable part of the Arab world, that its culture as well as its language is Arab, and that its orientation is to the East, not the West. Those who identify with the first position might well cultivate Israel as an ally and see the Palestinian refugees as intruders and as a hostile and dangerous presence; those at the other extreme might see the Palestinians as brothers to be assisted in every way and Israel as a hostile, imperialist Western enclave created to divide and to humiliate both Islam and the Arab world.

In general, and allowing for important exceptions, those most prone to the first identification would be the Maronites and those most prone to adopt the second identification, the Sunnites. Greek Catholics would place themselves closer to the first extreme; some Greek Orthodox would lean toward the second, others toward the first, as would be true of the Druzes, who perceive themselves to be a minority in Lebanon as well as in any possible united Syrian or Arab nation. Shi'ites, being Muslim, might identify with the second extreme, but warily and tentatively; like the Druzes, they feel themselves to be—and are often encouraged in this feeling—a minority in the Sunnite world about them. Armenians, Kurds, and Assyrians may be obedient citizens, but their dreams and their historical memories lie elsewhere. Other factors affecting identification are particular historical memories—the Sunnites, for example, resent the loss of the dominant position they enjoyed under the Ottomans—and particular traditional grievances—efforts by the Maronites, for example, to convert Greek Orthodox to their own faith.

Also of importance have been factors that encouraged integration by blurring the intensity of identification. One of these has been vested interests (in prosperity and in political status) that encouraged many prominent Muslims to accept the status quo and a substantial number of eminent and educated Maronites to accept Lebanon's presence in the Arab world and admit that it has an "Arab face." Christians who have held to this compromise position would argue that Lebanon's value is as a bridge between East and West, an interpreter of each to the other, and a transmitter of culture in both directions; they would take pride in Lebanon's multiethnicity and be in favor of toleration and sharing power—provided, of course, that Lebanon's sovereignty and the integrity of the Christian communities were not threatened. Such was the view of Michel Chiha, the principal author of Lebanon's constitution and the leading ideologue of Greater Lebanon at its inception.

Actual identification, as well as being conditioned by economic status, education, and level of sophistication, has also depended upon the positions taken by particular leaders in particular circumstances. Kamal Joumblatt, the eccentric and influential leader of an important segment of the Druzes, was the leader of the Progressive Socialist party; many of his followers, who were Druze peasants, supported him only because he was their *za'im* (traditional leader), not because they had dipped into the pages of *Das Kapital*. Another example is that of Antun Saadah, who attracted many Greek Orthodox to support his Syrian Social Nationalist party (PPS). This ideologue preached the idea of uniting all of historical Syria into one nation, with Cyprus included for geographical but not ethnic or historical reasons. His idea, still in vogue among some Lebanese, appealed to many Greek Orthodox because "Syria" was larger than Lebanon, which they perceive to be Maronite-dominated, and smaller than a united Arab nation, which they considered woud inevitably be Muslim in orientation. An Arab professor once said in the 1950s that had Saadah's first name been Muhammad rather than Antun he might have dominated the Arab world north of Egypt.

While it is true that many eminent Muslim leaders have paid only lip service to Pan-Arabism and to unlimited support for the Palestinians—this for electoral and political purposes—there has been and continues to be a broad cleavage in Lebanon between most Christians and most Muslims (even when the independence of Lebanon has not been at issue except by implication). Many Muslims have opposed the status quo for some of the following reasons: Christians, they maintain, have been the "haves"; they have controlled the most powerful levers of the state; and the state, as Greater Lebanon, has sovereignty over mainly Muslim areas that should have been part of Syria.

Over the years particular subjects of complaint have varied, but they have covered the social and political gamut, from minor—that Friday as well as Sunday should be a holiday, for example, or that the National Museum should include Muslim and Arab, as well as Phoenician and Roman, artifacts—to major. Among the latter three have been salient. One, Muslims have objected to the way power is distributed to enable Christians, particularly Maronites, to dominate a nation whose majority are Muslims. Power, it has been argued, should reflect population; thus, many Muslims have argued, it should be based, not upon sectarian distribution, but upon the principle of one vote for one person. A related objection has been the way the Christians have inflated their numbers by including as citizens emigrants, a majority of whom are Christian, and by readily giving citizenship to new Christian arrivals (the Armenians, for example) while refusing to do so for many Muslims (among them the Kurds and, more recently, Muslim Palestinians who might have wanted to become citizens).

Two, Muslims claim, the Christian establishment has repeatedly sought to split Lebanon, politically and culturally, from the Arab world. In the distant past, it has been observed, Maronites supported the Crusaders, and after World War I the Maronite patriarch (Ignatius Mubarak) had been explicit in his support of Zionism. Today, the "fascist" Kata'ib (the mainly Maronite Phalangist party) preaches separatism and hatred of Arabs. The very creation of Greater Lebanon, it has been asserted, was a case of "divide and rule" on the part of the Christian French and a repudiation of the desire of a majority of the Arabs for an Arab nation.

Three, Muslims argue, the Christian establishment has favored and promoted private and foreign education to the detriment of public education. This practice has served to erode the position of the Arabic language and has militated against Arab culture in general. Typically, Muslims say, many textbooks have belittled Arab accomplishments and promoted the image of Lebanon as once a Phoenician and now a Christian state. These complaints have often been expressed by Muslim community leaders; they found a particularly dramatic expression in a pamphlet entitled *Moslem Lebanon Today*, distributed in 1957, which was endorsed by a number of eminent Sunnite and Shi'ite leaders.

Christian responses to some of these objections and demands have included the following. Arab nationalism is inevitably "Muslim" in content and bias, and as Islam does not distinguish between church and state, only in Lebanon can Christians be first-class citizens; they need the guarantees the system affords. Furthermore, it has been argued, Muslims were hypocritical in calling for a secular state: They would never abandon their "personal status" (according to which matters of inheritance and marriage are determined by Koranic prescription). In addition, Lebanon has a historical mission that includes service to the Arabs and the Muslims as a bridge to modernity; only as an integral and separate entity can Lebanon perform this function. Integration to any degree of Lebanon politically or economically in the Arab world, with its authoritarian and socialist tendencies, would only jeopardize the freedom and prosperity that both Muslims and Christians enjoy in Lebanon. The realization of Muslim demands, in brief, would be killing the goose that laid the golden eggs, to nobody's benefit. Muslim leaders, Christians have claimed, know this and accept this; their public support for destructive attacks upon Lebanon is simply posturing for internal political purposes.

This discussion has presented extreme versions of views that are usually muted, but this dichotomy, or "schizophrenia," as some students of Lebanon have put it, is part of the explanation for the civil strife of 1958 and the disaster of 1975. The dichotomy—as well as the countervailing experience of compromise and mutual accommodation—has its origins in Lebanon's unique history. Both tendencies will undoubtedly be factors in whatever restructuring takes place after the Israeli invasion of 1982.

2

Formation

The intent in this chapter is to discuss the principal changes through which Lebanon has gone and to clarify important patterns or themes in the Lebanese experience that have repeated themselves, albeit each time in a novel shape and form.

TRANSFORMATIONS

Lebanon has experienced six transformations as an entity with some degree of structure and autonomy, seven if one includes the tragic and unpredictable situation since 1975, and eight if one includes the restructuring of the situation—both anarchic and stable—between 1978 and 1982. The ninth, to follow Israel's June 1982 invasion, has yet to take shape.

First, within the Ottoman Empire, a remarkable Druze ruler of the Ma'n family, Fakhr al-Din (1586–1635), created an autonomous principality—the amirate—which, at the time, included Beirut and the Biqa'. His court had important commercial connections with Italy, Tuscany in particular; his reign was marked by toleration and prosperity. He died at the hands of the Ottomans; subsequently the Muslim Shihab family (which later converted to the Maronite church) reconstituted the amirate (1697–1842) and by disguising their religious convictions won the support of both the powerful Druze and Maronite feudal lords. The most remarkable of the later amirs was Bashir II (1788–1840); under him the Mountain enjoyed genuine self-governance and, except for occasional eruptions of sectarian violence, provided for a liberal coexistence between the communal groups.

Second, on the heels of Napoleon's departure from Egypt, Muhammad 'Ali, that country's dynamic and aggressive pasha, and his son Ibrahim had by 1805 become a threat to the integrity of the Ottoman Empire itself; as they extended their sway against their Ottoman overlord, Lebanon came under Egyptian control for nine years (1831–1840).

17

Egyptian rule was flexible and tolerant; stability was provided, and education and commerce were promoted. At the same time, the West began to penetrate the region economically and, through missionary activity, culturally. Southern Lebanon, as William Polk has put it, was "opened" to Western modernity, as Egypt had been earlier by the Napoleonic invasion of 1798.[1]

One effect of this opening was that the Christians, until then second-class citizens, were able to assert themselves and become landlords and creditors as the Druze feudal lords were thrown on the defensive and held in check by the Egyptians. Christians and Druzes, however, unhappy over taxation and military recruitment, joined in rebellion against the Egyptians as the European powers, on their part, pressured Muhammad 'Ali to evacuate Syria. Once the Egyptians had left, the Druzes and the Maronites turned upon one another when Druze lords sought to reassert their fiscal privileges. The concert of major European powers thereupon intervened to impose a new transformation upon Lebanon, again within the ever-declining Ottoman Empire. This was the so-called Double Qaimaqamiate, which lasted from 1842 to 1860. The north was placed under Maronite command, the south under Druze command, with each ruler, or *qaimaqam*, subject to the Ottoman pasha of Sidon. The populations, however, overlapped, and many Maronite peasants continued to work for Druze overlords. When the northern Maronite peasantry, with the encouragement of their church, rebelled against their feudal lords in 1859, trouble was inevitable as dissidence spread among the Maronite peasants in the Druze area. An explosive situation led to the uprising of the Druze feudal lords, with the support of their coreligionists, against the Maronites. The Druze lords were encouraged by the Ottomans, and the powers gave support to one sect or another—the British, it was believed, to the Druze, the French to the Maronite. Terrible and widespread massacres, in which the Turks were also implicated, led to the death of about 11,000 Christians over a four-week period.

Again the powers intervened to establish Lebanon's fourth transformation, a regime under a non-Lebanese but Christian ruler, advised by an Administrative Assembly that represented the different sects according to number. The ruler was the *mutassarif*; the system, the Mutassarifiate, was given its constitutional structure between 1861 and 1864. This "Réglement Organique," or constitutional arrangement, abolished feudalism as a system of tax-gathering. Stability and experience in intercommunal parliamentary government on a limited scale were provided, but this entity, which did not include Beirut, was too small and too constricting for many Lebanese, who migrated in the hundreds to Egypt and to the Americas. Nevertheless, to judge from a common saying of the period, "Happy is he who has a shed for one goat in Mount Lebanon," life was tolerable enough.

During World War I, direct Ottoman rule was reimposed. Isolated even more than ever, the Mountain, and Lebanon in general, experienced an awful period of disease and hunger, sometimes even starvation.

After the war, Lebanon's life under the Ottomans came to an end as the Arab Territories of the empire came under Western control. The record of relations between the Lebanese and the Ottoman Turks had not been, overall, a very happy one. Ottoman rule had, however, permitted some autonomy to the Druzes and Maronites. Provided no trouble was caused and taxes were paid, Ottoman policy was to allow religious minorities to tend to their own affairs under the so-called *millet* system (a *millet* being a particular religious community).

The Ottoman Turks, Lebanon's overlords since the sixteenth century, initially could have imposed their will directly upon the Mountain. That they chose instead to allow the inhabitants of the Mountain a degree of autonomy—provided taxes were paid—was a matter of convenience. When *amirs* became too strong and independent in their behavior, direct intervention followed. Ottoman rulers were responsible, for example, for Fakhr al-Din's strangulation in 1635. But in the nineteenth century, as the Ottoman Empire lost its grip and Western intrusion into its affairs increased—consuls of the powers became very powerful—Ottoman authority in many of its provinces, including Lebanon, was weakened. In the sectarian conflicts among the Lebanese, as a result, Ottoman policy was often to encourage turbulence when Lebanese sects seemed unduly under the influence of one Western power or another, and Turkish commanders, implicitly and sometimes actively, supported their coreligionists against the Christians.

Under the Reform Movement, the *Tanzimat*, which was urged upon the declining Ottoman Empire by the West between the years 1839 and 1876, measures to provide Christians with greater legal equality were enacted; these often served to antagonize local Muslims. After the outbreak of World War I, however, when direct rule was imposed, maladministration encouraged a common hatred of the Turks, and a minority group of Christian and Muslim nationalists called for independence. This movement was suppressed, often brutally. In 1915–1916 some thirty-three Arab leaders, including some Christians as well as Druzes and Muslims, were publicly executed in Beirut and Damascus by the tough-minded governor, Djemal Pasha. A monument commemorating this common sacrifice stands at the Place des Martyres in downtown Beirut. (In 1981, a sad commentary on the times, the figures of the monument were decapitated.) To this day, Muslim and Christian Lebanese share one common myth, that the main source for the decline of Arab culture after the sixteenth century was the imposition of Turkish rule, a highly suspect historical thesis that unfortunately still poisons relations between Turks and Arabs. It did serve, however, to form a bond among the Lebanese.

After World War I, the sixth transformation came with the imposition of the French mandate over both Lebanon and Syria, a development opposed by all groups except the Maronite community, especially after the French proclaimed the establishment of Greater Lebanon in 1920. This decision, many Christians felt, would provide Lebanon with greater security and prosperity. Many Muslims were deeply resentful, as indicated earlier. To them the French, as Christians, were unwanted and, as Europeans, were imperialists.

Nevertheless, it was under the cloak of the mandate that the institutional framework and certain fundamental traditions for an independent Lebanon were elaborated. The Constitution was enacted in 1926 and revised in 1934. It was written mainly by the Maronite ideologue and businessman Michel Chiha; it provided for a republican presidential and (ultimately) unicameral system in which each community would enjoy representation according to its size. Pragmatically and wisely, a practice was adopted that became accepted as traditional: Sectarian tensions were reduced by providing that for each parliamentary seat competition would be intra- and not inter-confessional. The distribution of parliamentary seats, and for administrative posts, was to be in a ratio of six (Christians) to five (Muslims). The actual distribution was made final after the census of 1932, which has remained the basis for apportionment. To avoid the appearance of blatant bias toward the Maronites, the first president was a Greek Orthodox (Charles Debbas) elected in 1926, but as a number of Sunnite leaders who earlier had refused participation became reconciled to the system, the tradition became established that the president would be a Maronite (the first Maronite president took office in 1934), the prime minister a Sunnite (the first Sunnite prime minister took office in 1937), and the president of the Assembly a Shi'ite.

Of crucial importance for the future was the tradition established by an oral agreement, the National Pact, between the most prominent Maronite leader, Bishara Khuri, and Riad Sulh, his counterpart in the Sunnite community. According to this essentially negative but fundamental agreement, the Lebanese Christians would accept Lebanon's "Arab face" and refrain from any allegiance with a Western power; the Muslims, in turn, would agree to accept Lebanese sovereignty and refrain from seeking to merge Lebanon with any other part of the Arab world. Implicit was the understanding that the sectarian system of representation already evolved, based upon the 6 : 5 formula, would continue. The

Constitution was amended to read (Article 95): "Temporarily, and for the purpose of equity and amicable understanding, the Communities shall be represented in an equitable manner, in public offices and in the formation of the Cabinet, provided that this will not cause prejudice to the interests of the state." Although this seemed to contradict Articles 7 and 12, which provided for access to office on the basis of equality and without regard to sectarian distinctions, the logic was that sectarianism was only a provisional basis for distinction, one that time would eventually render unnecessary. The National Pact was never put into writing, but it was embodied in a speech made by Riad Sulh on October 7, 1943.[2]

On the whole, the French mandatory regime had both positive and negative features. The creation of Greater Lebanon, although it delighted many Christians, nevertheless populated the nation with primarily Muslim inhabitants whose allegiance was to "Syria" and to the "Arab nation" rather than to Lebanon. Also serving to alienate Muslims was the priority the French gave to the French language in education and administration and the special favors bestowed upon loyal Maronite politicians. Indignation among Muslims was also aroused by the harsh treatment of nationalists in neighboring Syria. Damascus was twice bombed by the French, in 1925 following an uprising and in 1945 as a futile measure to retain their evaporating hold on the Syrians. A Franco-Lebanese treaty drawn up after 1936 provided for the end of the mandate and for Lebanese independence. Because of opposition in the French Parliament, the treaty failed to be ratified.

There were some integrative features of French rule, however: the positive steps taken by the French to complete and to rationalize land registry, a process the Ottomans had started but had largely botched; the building of an infrastructure; the development of the nucleus of a modern army; and the enactment of the basic elements of the Lebanese political and administrative structure.

In addition, France encouraged integration negatively, albeit sometimes innocently and understandably, by exciting a common hostility against French rule. Tying the economy to the franc zone, for example, was perceived as exporting French problems to Lebanon, and France was blamed for failing to save the once lucrative silk industry from precipitous decline. (The real reasons had to do with international competition, from Japan in particular, and the decline could hardly have been avoided.) Another factor in encouraging common Lebanese resistance to the mandatory power were the indiscretions of one high commissioner, General Maurice Sarrail (1924–1925). A man of stubborn determination, he resorted to the first bombing of Damascus in 1925;

a fervent anticleric, he managed to antagonize even many francophile Maronites.

A final negative factor for integration was the graceless and even humiliating way the French managed their departure from Lebanon, as well as Syria, first under British and then under United Nations pressure. In 1943, following on the promise made by the Allies on June 8, 1941, after their landing against the Vichy regime earlier in the year, that Lebanon would henceforth be independent, the Lebanese parliament voted unilaterally to end the mandate. In response, French officials arrested a number of eminent Lebanese politicians, including the Muslim Riad Sulh and the Maronite Bishara Khuri, and so united many Muslims and Christians, the Maronite patriarch included, in a common desire to be rid of direct French control once and for all. Even if this did not break the sentimental and ideological attachment of many Christians to France, it did indicate that many Lebanese businessmen and political leaders were now convinced that national energies could best be developed in the context of independence. Last-ditch efforts by the French to maintain a military presence in Lebanon were defeated after Lebanon, a member of the United Nations in 1945, was able to rally international support to force the French to withdraw their last troops in December 1946.

A crucial factor making it possible for Christians and Muslims to take joint action against the French during this period was Khuri's victory in the presidential election of 1943 over Emile Iddi, the francophile Maronite leader most favored by the French. On the eve of the election of 1932, when Iddi won, H. S. Coold, U.S. consul general, wrote to Washington regarding Iddi's candidacy and his ideological point of view:

> In short, Edde will have no truck with Moslems. The Lebanon is a Christian country and, as far as the census figures, his attitude toward them (if they are ever published) will be precisely that of Admiral Farragut toward the torpedoes. I must modify this somewhat. M. Edde does recognize that there are now too many Moslems in this Christian refuge, and he is in favor of lopping off Tripoli and the extreme northern districts and presenting them to Syria, for the express purpose of getting rid of the objectionable community. Then he would consider the remaining Moslems as the Admiral considered the torpedoes or as the late Mr. Vanderbilt considered the public.[3]

One might observe that this thumbnail sketch of Iddi would, unfortunately, apply to many of his coreligionists. This is why, as Walid Khalidi and others have suggested, Khuri's victory in 1943 made Lebanon's sixth avatar a possibility. On January 8, 1944, the other Arab states recognized both Lebanon's sovereignty and its special status in the Alexandria Protocol as the Arab League came into being (March 22, 1945). Lebanon became a member of the league, and in the same year it was admitted to the United Nations.

THE LEBANESE AWAKENING

Before coming to Lebanon's final transformation—independence— a word should be said about the "Lebanese Awakening," a development running through the whole gamut of the metamorphoses discussed. This awakening was twofold: It involved, first, the mainly Maronite response to Western influence and, second, the contributions of Christians and Muslims alike to the broader "Arab Awakening" (the *Nahda*).

The Maronite link to the West goes back to the time of the Crusades, when these mountain Christians came to identify their destiny with that of the Christian Catholic West, Rome and France in particular. In 1584 a school was established in Rome to train Maronite priests (the Collegium Maronitarium), one of whose graduates, Butrus Mubarak, established the pattern for modern education when founding his school, 'Ayn Tura, in 1728. The first printing press, used mainly to publish religious and theological texts, had been introduced into Lebanon in 1610. As schools administered by Catholic missionaries proliferated and literacy became more widespread, the Maronites became the best-educated and thus the dominant sect in the Mountain.

In the early nineteenth century, however, the Catholic orders were to experience competition from Protestant missionaries from Europe and the United States. All benefited from this competition for the hearts and minds of the youth of Lebanon. In 1834 the American Press was established and in 1874 the Catholic Press. In 1866 the Syrian Protestant College was founded, to become the important regional university known after 1920 as the American University of Beirut (A.U.B.); in 1875 the Jesuit University of Saint Joseph was founded. Lebanon was becoming the most literate and best-educated (in Western terms) country in the Arab world. And increasingly Muslims, as well as Christians, were to seek entry into modernity through the educational network now available to them. In 1878, conscious of the relative underdevelopment of their communities, the Muslim Society of Benevolent Intentions (Jam'iyyat al-Maqasid al-Khayriyya al-Islamiyya) was established to provide, among other things, a modern education for Muslim youths.

The Arab Awakening involved the revival of classical Arabic as a medium of cultural intercourse and expression as well as the revival, in general, of the long-dormant Arab culture—with implications of Arab nationalism. Lebanon's role was pivotal. Lebanese immigrants helped to develop the modern press in Egypt, for example, and many of the important Arab essayists and creative writers who introduced and popularized Western ideas were Lebanese, among them Nasif Yaziji, Butrus Bustani, Faris Nimr, Yaqub Sarruf, and Salim and Bishara Taqla. By way of example, a few words might be said about one of the most outstanding of these cultural innovators, Butrus Bustani (1819–1883).

A scion of an educated Maronite family, he was trained at the seminary of 'Ayn Waraqa, after which he became associated with some of the newly arrived U.S. missionaries and converted to Protestantism. He helped in the important translation of the Bible undertaken by the Americans, a landmark in the foundation of a classical Arabic style marked by directness and simplicity. In 1863 he established his own institution, the National School, which emphasized Arabic and the sciences. Through the school, as well as in the dictionary and the encyclopedia he produced, he helped to adapt Arabic to serve as a vehicle for modern concepts. And in his magazine *Al-Jinan*, founded in 1870, he helped to popularize modern Western ideas and to advance the thesis that Arab civilization, which had once flourished, had long been in a state of decline and needed revival. Toward this goal, European ideas should be borrowed, among them the ideas of national unity and patriotism, as well as modern science. The patriotism he advocated was to "Syria," meaning the area populated by Arab-speaking people in today's Lebanon, Syria, Israel, and Jordan. His proto-nationalism, however, did not imply disobedience to the Ottoman Empire, and it did involve loyalty to an entity Christians could live comfortably in, an entity based upon individual equality and not upon religious divisions. Religion to him was creative only when it was free from any fanaticism. Later Christian writers advanced the idea of Arab nationalism but, like Bustani, never envisioned what many of them came, finally, to believe, that in any Arab nation Christians could only hope to be second-class citizens. In any case, men like Bustani were as important to the Arab Awakening as they were to the Lebanese Awakening.

In this context, the Syrian Protestant College made a contribution, through the translation of the Bible into Arabic as well as the publication of Arabic textbooks on modern subjects. Particular credit here goes to Cornelius Van Dyck, one of this institution's eminent professors. A.U.B. (and its predecessor), parenthetically, originally taught its subjects in Arabic; only later did it change to English to provide a more convenient access for its students to modern materials. Arab nationalists were later to argue that while this change in language may have helped raise standards, it also made this American education a force for alienation and cultural fragmentation. Whatever the case, A.U.B. and its rival Saint

TABLE 2.1   Presidencies

Charles Debbas	1926-1933
Habib al-Sa'd	1933-1935
Emile Iddi	1936-1941
Bishara Khuri	1943-1947
	1947-1952
Camille Chamoun	1952-1958
Fuad Shihab	1958-1964
Charles Hilu	1964-1970
Sulayman Franjiyya	1970-1976
Ilyas Sarkis	1976-1982
Amin Gemayel[a]	1982-

[a]Elected to replace Bashir
Gemayel, who was elected in 1982
but was killed before assuming
office.

Joseph have played a crucial role in helping to produce the "new men"
of the contemporary Arab world.

INDEPENDENT LEBANON: FACTORS FOR INTEGRATION AND FOR DISINTEGRATION

Independent Lebanon was, of course, heir to the experiences of
its earlier metamorphoses, and the past continues to form much of the
present. But since 1943, the Lebanese have had to meet the challenges
of their past on their own, without the support of the Concert of Powers
or of any one external power, be it Ottoman, Egyptian, or European.
The greatest challenge had become to maintain its sovereignty and its
integrity both against others and within itself. Some factors evident in
Lebanon's historical experience before independence have been favorable
to integration, others unfavorable.

One factor for integration over the centuries has been a remarkable
continuity in the complex of families that have led one sect or another
and provided Lebanon with some of its major leaders. In some cases
the descendants of yesterday's feudal chiefs are today's party leaders:
the Joumblatts and the Arslans among the Druzes; the Shihabs, Khuris,
and Iddis among the Maronites; the Sulhs and the Karamis among the
Sunnites; the Ussayrans and the 'Assads among the Shi'ites. Lebanon
is a small place, and these families have had long experience with each
other and with the rules and practices that make coexistence possible.

Conversely, one could argue that the persistence of such traditionalism among the Lebanese reveals an underlying inflexibility that can inhibit experimentation and the adoption of fresh approaches.

Providing for both stability and relative political immobility, on the other hand, has been the rule of the game, persisting through Lebanon's historical experience, that issues never be pushed to their extreme, that they be resolved through compromise and give and take. It was to preserve this balance that Lebanon has supported the Arab side in wars with Israel but in fact never seriously become engaged. In 1948 Lebanon went to war against Israel but not very actively—the armistice of March 1949 still determines the border between them. In 1956 Lebanon did not even break off diplomatic relations with France and Great Britain when they, together with Israel, invaded Egypt. In 1967, so strong was the outrage in Lebanon over the (unfounded) accusation that U.S. and British planes had helped Israel destroy the Egyptian air force that the ambassadors of the United States and the United Kingdom were asked to leave, but only for a short time. In 1973 Lebanon provided some logistic support to Syria, but the Lebanese army did not participate in the war. It was because they accepted the rule of everything in moderation that Bishara Khuri and Riad Sulh were effective leaders, and it was because he was seen as violating this rule that Camille Chamoun brought grief to his nation in 1958. The civil strife of that year deserves special consideration because during it masks were removed and screens covering political realities in normal times were drawn back.

In broad strokes, the ruler of Egypt, Nasser, by nationalizing the Suez Canal Company in 1956 and by surviving the subsequent invasion by Israel, Great Britain, and France, had emerged as the most popular Arab leader for decades if not centuries. Enthusiasm for him, and hopes for the creation under him of the Arab state that had so far proved elusive had swept the Arab world, including Lebanon; and when Syria and Egypt united in 1958, the basis for this state seemed to have been established. In many parts of Lebanon his picture was on proud display; the flag of the United Arab Republic was occasionally waved provocatively in street demonstrations, and prominent Muslims defiantly visited Damascus upon Nasser's visit to offer their congratulations. At the same time the United States was in the process of building an alliance, the so-called Baghdad Pact, as a shield against the USSR. Earlier Lebanon had refused to join the Baghdad Pact, but by 1958 President Chamoun, supported by many Lebanese who now feared for Lebanon's sovereignty, had decided that firm action was needed to counter the appeal of Nasser. When President Eisenhower offered his "doctrine," according to which the United States would help defend any government threatened with communist subversion, Lebanon accepted it, the only Arab state to do so. As a reward, Lebanon received a $20 million assistance package.

This seemed to many of Chamoun's opponents to be a repudiation of the National Pact, as had the elections of 1957 in which, by government pressure and through various electoral devices, Chamoun had ensured the defeat of some of his most eminent Muslim and Druze opponents, including Kamal Joumblatt and two men who have often been prime ministers, Sa'b Salam and Abdallah Yafi. At the same time, Chamoun also upset the balance by keeping as his prime minister the loyal Sami al-Sulh, a pro-Western politician with little real following, a decision that was interpreted as denying Muslims adequate representation in the governance of the country. And to top it all, Chamoun was believed to covet a second term as president.

On May 8, 1958, after the assassination of an anti-Chamoun journalist (a Maronite, in fact), the opposition, organized as the United National Front, set up barricades and manned their various fiefdoms and city quarters. Clashes occurred; there were only a few small battles and about 2,000 to 4,000 casualties, but the legitimacy of the government had been challenged, and anarchy threatened the society. Fortunately, cooler heads prevailed; the commander of the army, General Fuad Shihab, refused to involve his troops, and the Maronite patriarch, Boulos Meouchy, remained in opposition to Chamoun, as did ex-president Bishara Khuri. Chamoun and his supporters were thrown on the defensive. After the overthrow of the pro-Western monarchy in Iraq in July, consternation both in Lebanon and in Washington led to the landing of 10,000 U.S. Marines to help establish stability in Beirut and elsewhere. But Chamoun, although he was able to complete his term in office, did not seek a second term, and General Shihab was elected president. The U.S. Marines then left in response to an Arab-sponsored resolution in the U.N.

At first Shihab failed to act in the spirit of the National Pact— he appointed a cabinet (with Rashid Karami as prime minister) too heavily weighted toward the opposition, and the Christian Kata'ib, with its well-organized paramilitary units, called for a strike and closed down Beirut. Matters were adjusted, however, when a new cabinet of "salvation" that included the leader of the Kata'ib, Pierre Gemayel, as well as Raymond Iddi, was appointed (Karami remained as prime minister). The National Pact was given a new lease on life, and the civil war was declared to be over according to the formula "neither victors nor vanquished." Chamoun and his supporters maintain that by his extreme actions he had saved Lebanon; his opponents claim that he had threatened the nation with disintegration. But in any case, the "events," as they were called, had shown both the fragility of the system and the need in crisis (as on several occasions in the past) to rely upon a foreign power or powers to intervene to help restore the balance. At the same time the final resolution of the crisis showed that enough Lebanese appreciated the need for moderation and compromise as a condition for Lebanese integration to make the system work.

Another factor making for integration has been the rise of a prosperous middle class with transsectarian vested interests. Members of this class are often allied through business partnerships, especially in the city of Beirut. As early as the middle of the nineteenth century such people were playing an important political role—for example, the Ottoman authorities, not without some cause, accused a committee of Beirut businessmen of having encouraged, in 1858–1859 the repudiation by the Maronite peasantry of feudalism, so helping to foment the disruptive events that led to the 1860 massacre. It was this class that sanctioned the strike in 1952, in an economic climate of inflation and unemployment, that helped force Bishara Khuri, accused of corruption and nepotism, to resign from his position as second-term president in the so-called perfumed revolution of 1952. And it was this class that supported the renewal of the terms and spirit of the National Pact in 1958.

An outstanding member of this Beirut mercantile class has been the octogenarian Henri Pharaon, one of the richest men in Lebanon, a banker, the owner of the port of Beirut, a brilliant political broker, an aesthete whose mansion contains a fabulous collection of works of art, and a fervent defender of laissez-faire. Pharaon has been involved, directly or indirectly, with the life of the republic since its beginning, both as a performer and as a devoted defender. He has consistently argued that the Lebanese nation can thrive only if moderation, compromise, and accommodation between the different sects prevail. Any attempt to push the nation in any extreme direction, he has insisted, can only be perilous. This was the position he maintained in his articles and books (for example, *Au Service du Liban et son unité* [in service to Lebanon and its unity] [1959], a collection of articles that appeared originally in the Beirut newspaper *Le Jour*); this was the position that he took in defending the National Pact of 1943, which he helped draft. And it was in this spirit that he contributed to preventing the Pact of the Arab League (1944–1945) from becoming a binding alliance—which would have contradicted the National Pact—and that in 1958, as a member of the "Third Force," a coalition of those who favored neither side, he opposed President Chamoun and helped resolve the conflict. A Greek Catholic from an old mercantile family and brother-in-law of Michel Chiha, Lebanon's founding ideologue, Pharaon, like other businessmen of his ilk, has been both an architect and a guardian of Lebanon's integrity as a liberal open and capitalist society.

But this same class is also a disintegrative factor insofar as its often blatant commitment to money-making and to the laissez-faire ethic has served as a barrier to needed social reforms and, because of its mainly mercantile composition, to the progress of industry in Lebanon. This class also showed insufficient sensitivity to the fact that as Beirut prospered and expanded, dangerous slums came into being—the Basta, the Armenian bidonvilles along the Beirut River, and the "poverty belt" on the outskirts of the city. The potential for anomie now existed, and among particular confessional groups, the Shi'ites in particular, there was the mounting resentment that it was from their number that the slum-dwellers came. The first battles of the Civil War of 1975 were to break out in the impoverished areas of Maronite 'Ayn al-Rummana and Shi'ite al-Shayyah. Modernization, as has been often observed, can be disintegrative if the benefits of progress are shared unequally among the different social components. In Lebanon, in particular, class grievance and sectarian feeling can blend to form a dangerous brew.

Another important factor for integration has been the Lebanese wont to accept newly arrived groups and to allow them to participate in the system; this has been true of the Armenians and of the Greek Orthodox who fled from Damascus during the massacre of 1860. On the other hand, the unwillingness of the establishment to allow other groups into the polity—some Kurds, some poorer Muslims in the northern Akkar region, and most important, the Palestinians—has proved disintegrative. Until 1965, while Palestinians who were better educated entered into the business and the academic worlds, and some Christians among them even into the polity as citizens, the bulk remained in the camps, which were only routinely supervised. Bishara Khuri had welcomed them initially and offered them at least temporary haven. But after 1965 the Palestinians came to be seen increasingly as militant and aggressive and dangerously allied to Lebanese leftist parties who sought radical change in the system or to parties that preached transnational goals (or both). Clashes occurred between army and Palestinian units in 1969, and the situation continued to deteriorate, especially after King Hussein of Jordan expelled the armed Palestinian units from Jordan (1970–1971) and left Lebanon as the only place where the Palestine Liberation Organization (PLO) could continue to maintain armed bases close to Israel (in Syria and Egypt the Palestinian refugees were kept under strict control). By 1965 the Palestinian factor was to play a critical role in the disintegration that culminated in the events of 1975.

Ironically, another factor for disintegration is Lebanon's inevitable commitment to liberty—inevitable because no one national component

Palestinian refugees, 1980. (Credit: Mark Lane)

has been strong enough to dominate the others. To exist Lebanon has had to commit itself, even if only hypocritically, to free institutions and to a modicum of participation in the polity by all the various confessional groupings. This may have saved Lebanon from authoritarianism, but it has made for a "porous" nation, as it has sometimes been described, one unable to exclude or to effectively counteract foreign influence and intrusion. Thus, for example, while Lebanon has enjoyed the freest press among the Arab states, and in spite of the high quality of some of its newspapers, this press has been subject to venal corruption and to foreign subvention. As early as the eighteenth century, foreign travelers remarked upon the atmosphere of liberty in Lebanon, and rightly so. It was partly this liberty that made the Lebanon of yesterday so compelling, but in so fragmented a society, it also constituted a danger to the nation's cohesion.

Yet, dangerous as liberty may be when it turns into anarchy, it can also be a force for integration if it is protected from excess by the appropriate institutions and if it is accepted as a positive value and sustained by consensus. It is this liberty, which many Lebanese were so proud of, that will be explored in the following chapters.

NOTES

1. William Polk, *The Opening of South Lebanon, 1788–1840* (Cambridge, Mass.: Harvard University Press, 1963).

2. See *Le Jour,* Beirut, October 8, 1943, and excerpts in *Middle East Forum* (Beirut), January 1959, p. 6.

3. Dated April 4, 1932, in Walter L. Browne, *The Political History of Lebanon, 1920–1950. Documents on Politics and Political Parties Under French Mandate, 1920–1936* (Salisbury, N.C.: Documentary Publications, 1976), Vol. 1, p. 150.

3

Society

In spite of its regional, class, and sectarian disparities, Lebanon was relatively prosperous and modern before 1975, and for most people, natives and visitors alike, it was a pleasant place to live and to work.

Lebanon's society, like that of other Mediterranean and Arab lands, was a variegated, complex one, full of obvious contrasts of the modern and the traditional. One needed only compare the traditionalist Muslim atmosphere of Tripoli and Sidon with Beirut's cosmopolitanism, or the impoverished periphery of Beirut with its districts with luxury hotels, beaches, and cabarets. Nevertheless, it also had a common ambience, a unity of sorts, because of the importance of Beirut (with some 40 percent of the population, and easy access to most parts of the country by bus and by "service," or group taxis), the symbiosis between villages and cities, and even, paradoxically, the pattern of sectarianism itself, a visible reality, a source sometimes of humor. As Paul Starr has observed,[1] compartments were not airtight; for political convenience, in part, the Muslim Shihabs became Maronites in the eighteenth century, and it could happen that a Sunni would become a Shi'ite to allow his daughter to inherit an estate, a Maronite become a Greek Orthodox to divorce, or a member of any other sect become a Maronite in order to be a candidate for president!

Identifications and loyalties, as discussed earlier, are to the sect; on a more intimate and immediate level they are to the extended family more than to either state or class. The sense of family honor (ird) is of paramount importance. Traditional values are distantly rooted in those of the now disappearing Beduin: hospitality, protection of the guest, male prowess, vengeance when called for. And the values of the village, where kinship ties are strong and identity is communal, continue to form the basis for the socialization of most Lebanese. These values, often called "primordial," can be negative from the point of view of the state; yet in terms of psychological and sometimes physical security, they provide for a sense of rootedness, a comfortable feeling of belonging.

LEBANON

The Lebanese extended family is the basic unit of society, and the lineage kinship networks serve to mediate between the individual and the larger social units and the state. In the rural areas the extended family is the important productive unit, and in the towns and cities productive units are most often owned and run by a family unit: Yusif Sayigh has estimated that of 1,861 manufacturing and mining units (in the Industrial Census of 1955), 1,129 (60.6 percent) were under single ownership, 694 (37.3 percent) were partnerships, and only 38 (2 percent) were corporations (mostly banking and money exchange enterprises).[2] Typically, the concentration of employees in a business has been along family, ethnic, and religious lines.

The extended family provides many services to the individual, as Samih Farsoun has pointed out.[3] Because of trust among its members, the family is a source of investment capital; it is a support for education (a kinship group often will collaborate to educate a promising young relation to carry on the family business, for example); it is a medium for obtaining employment; it serves the function of a bank; through migration and success abroad it is a source of remittances; and in times of crisis it can provide refuge and in times of illness and of old age, social security.

The Lebanese have been accused of being "levantines," bicultural or multicultural persons with flexible and adaptable morals; but the fierce cohesion within hostile communities during the Civil War might be taken as evidence that most Lebanese were not levantines. This does not mean that many Lebanese have not been prone to materialism and to a healthy appetite for pecuniary gain and conspicuous consumption, often preferring to make their mark in trade and services rather than in more productive areas such as agriculture and industry. Distance from traditionalist values increases, as one might expect, with education and exposure to modernity. But what is remarkable with the Lebanese case is the extent to which the primordial has survived and in some ways even been reinforced by modernization and urbanization.

MODERNIZATION

One clear indication of Lebanon's change toward modernity has been the status and the condition of women. Feminine visibility—as represented by the veil or by the absence of women from cafes—has been lowest in the less modernized communities and classes. So also have been the number of women employed and the degree of premarital consultation, that is, the degree to which spouses were acquainted or were consulted as to their wishes before marriage; the gap in age between spouses, on the other hand, has been highest in such communities.

The trend has been toward greater "modernity," by which is meant in the present context a movement from the extended to the nuclear family, more employment and education for women, a growing approximation of the ages of spouses, and an increasing possibility for women to divorce as easily as men. This trend has been observed among both Christians and Muslims, with the Christians, because of their earlier and deeper exposure to the West, having a slight edge.

It has also been observed of both groups that the "achievement ethic" has increasingly been cultivated among the young, as also the tendency to adopt child-rearing practices that operate to weaken the cultivation of an "authoritarian personality." E. T. Prothro and Lutfy Diab,[4] as well as others, have offered evidence to show that Lebanon

TABLE 3.1   Comparative Modernization

	Literacy (1973)	PQLI (1973)	GNP per capita (1974)	No. of Daily Newspapers (1965)
Lebanon	86%	80	$1,070	120[a]
Syria	40%	52	$ 560	21
Egypt	26%	46	$ 280	15
Iraq	26%	46	$1,160	12
Jordan	32%	48	$ 430	11
Saudi Arabia	--	--	--	3
(Israel)	(84%)	(90)	($3,460)	

Sources: Adapted from James Bill and Carl Leiden, Middle East Politics (Boston: Little, Brown, 1979); Michael Hudson, The Precarious Republic: Modernization in Lebanon (New York: Random House, 1968).

follows what appears to be a worldwide trend, from the patrilinear, patriarchal, endogamous, and sometimes polygamous to the Western pattern. The trend has been strongest in Beirut, but it has been identifiable in the rural areas also. Easy divorce for men and polygamy (in Islam, men are allowed up to four wives) have slowly been declining; increasingly women have instituted divorce proceedings, married outside the family, shed veils, practiced birth control, had smaller families, received education, and become employed. In the 1970s several thousand women were employed in Tripoli, a conservative Muslim city, and in Beirut women have been very visible in offices, teaching positions, and even, in one case, in parliament. Emancipated women like Leila Baalbaki have written novels denouncing the prejudice against women that continues to prevail. Marriage is still subject to sectarian religious considerations; there is no civil marriage in Lebanon.

Nevertheless, not only in regard to women, but in general, Lebanon has been in the vanguard in the modernizing of the Arab world, judging by the indices employed by sociologists—Daniel Lerner's "empathy," for example; or Karl Deutsch's social mobility, size of media audience, literacy, urbanization (40 percent in Lebanon), or percentage of population in services (40 percent in Lebanon), which Michael Hudson has applied to Lebanon; or a composite index of all these, the Physical Quality of Life Index (PQLI), made use of by James Bill and Carl Leiden[5] (see Table 3.1).

One might expect that one feature of the process of modernization would be a decline in sectarian identification, but if students of the subject like Samir Khalaf are right, this does not necessarily happen.

Certainly it has not happened in the case of Lebanon. It has been observed of the 1970s, for example, that in Beirut, in some ways a melting pot, those who moved from the villages into the city tended to reside where their coreligionists did and to enter trades associated with one sect or another. Sixty-nine percent of the Armenians in Beirut, for example, lived around the Beirut River; 79 percent of the Sunnites in and around the central area known as the Basta; and some 75 percent of the Maronites in Ashrafiyyah in east Beirut, in and around 'Ayn al-Rummana. Sectarianism has not only persisted, but as Fuad Khuri and others have argued, it has been more important than class consciousness and has served to blunt class identification.[6]

Class divisions exist and are locally recognized, but they tend to be based more upon factors of family status and prestige than upon income. A person who owns his own business, however humble this might be, has more status than an employee of someone else, even though the latter may have a higher income. In his study of the town of Amyun, Khuri found that the inhabitants themselves perceived the class structure to include four levels: notables whose families have been community leaders for at least three generations; the affluent; the notable poor (a taxi driver who owns his own car, for example); and the needy (peasants, for example, who work for others). It required one generation to rise from the bottom to the next two levels; three generations to rise to the top.

Another classification sometimes made, more relevant to a more traditionalist and less mobile society, such as in the largely Shi'ite south, has been to divide the population into the "learned families" (about 20 percent in the south), who are the large landholders; the small traders; and the peasants. Until recent times, fealty by the peasants to the upper class had been accepted without question. In general, in Lebanon, organizations that depend upon a degree of class consciousness, in the Marxist sense, have been weak.

Before 1975, for example, although trade unions were becoming increasingly important and strikes frequently occurred, the largely Christian and moderate union leadership had accepted the Lebanese system, and generally unions did not take a political stand, even though the Communist party supported one of their federations. Membership was small; licensed unions, which in 1974 numbered 169, organized into nine labor confederations, included about 57,000 members, only 15 percent of the nonagricultural labor force. In the case of many small family industrial enterprises, unions had difficulty penetrating because employers relied on members of the extended family and upon fellow sectarians. The Lebanese work force, about 572,000, or 27 percent of the population in 1971, was very poorly educated; about 50 percent had only an elementary education and some 30 percent were illiterate. Agricultural workers were not organized at all; illiteracy among them was about 93 percent.

A number of important associations whose orientation is professional have been important to an extent in transcending sectarianism. Among these are the Beirut and Tripoli bar associations (with some 1,800 members), the Lebanese Association of Architects and Engineers (3,500), and the Lebanese Medical Association (1,400). Other groups have included the Lebanese Chamber of Commerce, the Lebanese Manufacturers Association, and the politically influential Lebanese Merchants Association. In these and similar associations, Christians have tended to predominate among the leadership. An interesting proposal, sometimes publicly discussed, is to increase national cohesion by having representatives from these essentially professional and nonsectarian associations elected to serve as a second parliamentary chamber.

In addition to sectarian identification, a check to pressures that might make for class war has been migration, a particular wont of the Lebanese. Migrants, when successful abroad as many Lebanese have been, have helped to support their families at home through remittances. One estimate has it that in the 1910s such remittances constituted as much as 41 percent of Lebanon's foreign earnings. Not infrequently, the successful emigrant would return to his village to marry a local girl or to retire with his capital. Between 1860 and 1900, 3,000 Lebanese migrated each year; between 1900 and 1914, 15,000 per year; and between 1951 and 1959, 2,850 per year. By 1970 there were probably more than 1 million Lebanese migrants overseas. Most of the emigrants have been Christians, the plurality of these Maronites; the main reason for migration has been economic. Since 1975, however, some half million Lebanese have chosen to live abroad because of the internal chaos, although some were economically motivated by employment possibilities in the oil-rich Gulf states. The latter, again, feed the Lebanese economy with remittances, but on the negative side migration now constitutes a talent drain.

There is some truth to Kamal Joumblatt's rather sardonic description of the typical Lebanese emigrant, although, of course, it ignores the thousands who became fully assimilated, and usually prosperous, in the lands to which they migrated:

> Depatriation doesn't change them much. It is said that a Lebanese who migrates takes three things with him which he clings to as if they were family heirlooms: first of all his concern for personal dignity [wajaha], that is for everything that can give him the air of a bourgeois; second, his village accent which he preserves even in Spanish or English; finally,

his fanaticism regarding his home-town. To this baggage one can add three other things: the hollow-rock in which he makes *kibbeh*—he's a good eater—his preoccupation with his own personal interest, and his taste for back-backbiting [gossip]. . . . On their return after thirty or fifty years they are just as they left.[7]

Internal migration to the cities has also been an important phenomenon. Some villagers have been attracted by jobs, others have fled because of danger—Maronites during the event of 1860, Shi'ites more recently because of Israeli retaliatory raids. Cities have expanded, and the nonurban population by 1975 was only about 30 percent.

CITY AND VILLAGE

Crucial in Lebanon's life has been Beirut; in 1970, 70 percent of all industrial laborers and 60 percent of those engaged in services worked there, and by 1975 the city included at least 40 percent of the population. A major city and legal center during the time of the Romans, it began to decline after an earthquake in 551 A.D. Although it underwent temporary revivals, as under Fakhr al-Din in the seventeenth century, in the first decades of the nineteenth century it was still only a harborless town of some 8,000, lit by olive oil, accessible from the sea to goods and passengers only on the backs of sturdy harbormen. With the arrival of the missionaries, the favorable atmosphere under the Egyptian occupation, and increasing penetration into the area by industrial Europe, it began to flourish. By 1850, with a population of some 45,000, it was joined to Istanbul by telegraph, to Europe by seven steamships that made regular calls, and to Damascus by a road opened by the French Damascene Road Company. French and Italian, as well as Arabic, could be heard in its streets. By this time levantines of mixed culture and enterprising ways and "compradors," or local agents of foreign companies, had become a feature of the urban scene.

By 1920, when Beirut became capital of Greater Lebanon under the French, about 40 percent of its population consisted of Sunnites, 28 percent of Greek Orthodox, 25 percent of Maronites, and 7 percent of Greek Catholics. These were soon joined by newly arrived Armenian refugees from Turkey. In the 1940s, Shi'ites from the south began to enter Beirut in large numbers; these multiplied after the 1950s when the south increasingly became a battlefield between Israel and the Palestinians. As foreign schools were opened and international companies established regional bases in the city, the number of expatriates grew: one estimate is that in 1975 there were about 15,000 Americans, 14,000 British, and 30,000 French in Beirut. The non-Lebanese may have

Beirut street scene in the 1960s. (Credit: Grace Thomas)

constituted as much as half the population. Included were 350,000 Syrian residents and 315,000 transients, 370,000 Palestinians, 75,000 Egyptians, and 78,000 from elsewhere in Africa.

As early as 1906, when its population reached 120,000, Beirut had already become an important cultural center, with its two universities, fifteen printing houses, and its twelve Arabic-language newspapers. In the boom years of the 1950s the population rose to 700,000. Since independence the number of banks had risen from 5 to 936. In 1970 Beirut boasted 260 private schools, fifty-six public schools, and four universities. With its dens of entertainment and vice of all sorts, as well as its cultural resources, it could claim to be a Paris (even if a provincial one); and with its polyglot and polycultural complexity, a Babel. The scene included solemn, and often political, Friday mosque sermons as well as sophisticated lectures in French at the Cénacle Libanais; the mainly Maronite Gallic atmosphere of Saint Joseph as well as the American atmosphere of the American University of Beirut, with its students from many other Arab and Third World countries as well as Lebanon; and talented Armenian violinists playing Chopin as well as popular Arab poets reading their works to massive and enthusiastic audiences.

Beirut, to radical intellectuals, was the capital of degenerate and exploitative capitalism; to many Arab nationalists, its cosmopolitanism was a repudiation of Arab culture. To the rich of other Arab countries, it was a delight, a place where they could enjoy the West in an Arab ambience; to Arab political victims of coups and revolutions, a place where they could find haven and still keep touch with their peoples. For many foreigners it was the last of the major free Mediterranean polycultural ports of the Orient, once Tangier and Alexandria had been absorbed into their respective hinterlands.

Each quarter of Beirut has had its own particular ethos, its particular sectarian critical mass, and links with villages have persisted and provided many with psychological roots as well as a source of cheap food; yet Beirut, although prosperous, has had its slums and its mobs, rendered the more dangerous because of underlying religious passions. Albert Hourani once wrote of "the great, growing, rootless community of the Levantine city" that "might lie open to sudden gusts of political passion springing from a submerged religious feeling." Beirut had become one such city. After 1975, Beirut became on occasion as divided as Berlin, with the mainly Christian east and the mainly Muslim west roughly separated by the Beirut-Damascus road and the "Green Line" that one crosses at one's peril in times of confrontation. And, of course, many districts had been destroyed, and financial and industrial activity were often brought to a halt.

Before 1975 Beirut, however, was home to many international companies that favored it because of its freedom, the availability of talented personnel that was polyglot, and the relative efficiency of its infrastructure. Also centered in Beirut, a tribute to the entrepreneurship of the Lebanese, have been some of the most imaginative and efficient Lebanese companies, among these Middle East Airlines, Trans-Mediterranean Airways, and the Contracting and Trading Company. Undaunted even by the chaos of the Civil War, many such companies continued to operate and to keep their shattered nation on the map.

While Beirut was the ganglion of the nation—as were the coastal cities of Sidon, Tyre, and Tripoli and the inland city of Zahlah to a lesser extent—the villages and towns of the Mountain played an important economic and social role as centers of local trade, places for voting in parliamentary elections, summer resorts, and places for relaxation and renewal for those living in the cities. As Samir Khalaf and Per Kongstad concluded in their study of pre–Civil War Rue Hamra, one of Beirut's most prosperous shopping centers, urbanites tended to congregate among their own and to keep close ties to their villages, both physically and in regard to values—a check to city anomie, Khalaf and Kongstad maintain.[8] Most villages were not isolated; cheap transportation tied them to the cities, and through remittances from departed

Ain Mreissie in Beirut, depicting different styles of architecture. (Credit: Donna Egan)

sons (and sometimes the return of these sons) many villages reached out well beyond Lebanon to Africa and the Americas. Some of the towns—Aley, Bhamdoun, Broummana, and others—would become mini-capitals during the summer, when their hotels, casinos, and cabarets attracted tourists from many parts of the Arab world; and before the collapse of 1975, Baalbeck in the Biqa' provided spectacular international and Arab festivals amid its massive Roman ruins. Yet because Beirut had become so predominant in the national economy, and because banking and medical facilities were attracted to it, the rest of the country was at a disadvantage. Doctors were hard to come by, and the lack of banking facilities encouraged hoarding or borrowing from local usurers, both a source of instability and a block to capital accumulation and investment.

LITERARY AND INTELLECTUAL LIFE

Although provincial and derivative in some ways and dominated almost exclusively by Beirut, cultural life in Lebanon before the Civil War was lively and variegated. Because of the hospitality of the Lebanese, their humor and their liberality, the ambience was attractive and often stimulating. Besides the resorts, the cabaret reviews, and the more babylonian pleasures Beirut had to offer, there was abundant food for the intellect. The international press, and books from Paris, London, and New York as well as Baghdad, Damascus, and Cairo, were readily available. Cultural issues were discussed in reviews of quality—*al-Hikma*, *Al-Adab*, *Al-Adib*, and *Al-Abhath*—as well as in the more serious newspapers—*Al-Nahar*, *L'Orient*, and *Le Jour* (the last two have been amalgamated as *L'Orient-Le Jour*). Theater was available in Arabic, French, English, and Armenian and on stages where *chansonniers*, in the French style, would satirize the events and personalities of the day. Music of high quality—classical, Arabic, and folkloric—could be heard at different concert halls and at spectacles such as the Baalbeck festival in summer. Lectures in Arabic, French, and English could be attended on university campuses and at cultural centers such as the Cénacle Libanais. Also attractive was the spontaneous culture one found at gatherings (*haflas*) at which guests might easily break into improvised dialogues in poetry or recitations of the classical writers, or the whole assembly might dance the *debke*, the traditional round dance.

On the surface, and to the casual visitor, the atmosphere might appear casual, insouciant, and relaxed, but as has become evident, beneath this surface there were serious, even ominous tensions and anxieties, and issues were discussed and debated that could become explosive and help turn this Mediterranean forum into a slaughterhouse.

Among such issues, as will be discussed, were questions of language—whether Lebanon could afford to continue to be polyglot—and of historiography—how to view the Lebanese past. Related issues of equal visceral import, in the literary and intellectual ethos, had to do with the question of Lebanon's identity, whether this identity was or should be "Western" or "Eastern" or some combination of the two—expressed poetically, whether Lebanon was the creature of the desert or of the Mediterranean Sea.

Some issues important to Lebanon's intellectuals and artists are common to the Arab world, or even the Third World as a whole; some are shared with the Western world, France in particular; and some are specific to this small crossroads buffeted by so many currents. The discussion that follows will focus mainly but not exclusively upon orientations among Christians, because they have been on the whole positively rather than negatively involved in the "ideology" of Lebanon as it was constituted in 1920. For most, although certainly not all, Muslims, the important centers of thought and creativity lie outside Lebanon, in Damascus and Cairo, for example.

A subject of perennial concern and debate has been whether Lebanon can or should separate itself from the sweep of Arab nationalism and its values and goals. To this movement the Lebanese, including many Christians, have contributed a great deal, as already seen, and Beirut has played an important role in the *Nahda*, the renaissance of Arab culture and of the Arabic language. Some Christian Lebanese, particularly among the Greek Orthodox, have had no trouble in supporting the cause of Arab nationalism, although some, as in the case of Antun Saadah and the Pan-Syrian movement, have qualified this support by basing their ideology upon geographical rather than religious considerations and upon a vision of the past rooted in the pre-Islamic era, the Seleucid period in particular.

Among Maronites who supported independence from the Ottoman Empire in the early twentieth century, who took pride in Arabic culture and language, and who talked of liberation and self-determination for the Arabs, on the other hand, there was a tendency to think of any "Arab nation" in purely Western terms, as liberal, parliamentary, secular, and constitutional and based upon the Rights of Man. Later on this prospect was to dim, but at the time it appeared to be the wave of the future. Others, more skeptically, agreed to the ideal of Arab liberation, provided that Lebanon's "special personality" be recognized and provided for. And still others, of course, were interested exclusively in full independence for Lebanon itself. There have been, in addition to these three groups, Christian intellectuals and ideologues who have never made up their minds or who, for reasons of political opportunism, wear several hats depending upon the context in which they find themselves.

One early Christian pioneer of Arab nationalism, often mentioned in essays and anthologies on Arab nationalism, was Negib Azoury, author of *La réveil de la nation arabe* [The awakening of the Arab nation] (1905), a book only recently translated into Arabic. The position adopted by Azoury illustrates the ambivalence of some of these early Christian Arab nationalists. Although he was deeply anti-Ottoman, foresaw and warned against the settlement of Jews in Palestine, and advocated Arab liberation and the creation of an Arab state (in his case exclusive of Egypt, which he saw as having its own ethos), he nevertheless proposed that this new nation be under the aegis of France! At about the same time Bulus Nujaym, under the pen name "M. Jouplain," published *La question du Liban* [The question of Lebanon] (1908), a book much more in keeping with the sentiments of most Maronites. In it he advocated the creation of Greater Lebanon, anticipating what France was, in fact, to establish in 1920. His argument was that for the country to be viable, and for the Christians to be secure, Lebanon should reach to the borders it had enjoyed on occasion in the past—as under Fakhr al-Din, for example—and include Beirut. It is this strictly Lebanese nationalist orientation that underlies the ideology of the Gemayels and the Chamouns and that today flourishes in Jounieh and in Kaslik—although some now wonder if Greater Lebanon, which diluted Christian numerical superiority, had been such a good idea after all.

Other Christian ideologues, many of whom express their views in French at the Cénacle Libanais, among them Michel Chiha and René Habashi, have expressed this Lebanese idea with greater nuance than the more extremist Christians, but the vision is the same. Appeals are made for a dialogue with Islam through which it is hoped Arabist ideologues can be convinced that Lebanon is also theirs and that it serves as a conduit for modernization and progress not only for Lebanon but for the whole Arab world. There is also talk of a "Mediterranean civilization" or "mentality" of which the Lebanese, even while recognizing the "Arab face" of Lebanon, partake. On occasion, on the podium of the Cénacle Libanais, however, one might hear remarks hardly conducive to dialogue with Islam—for example, when one *conférencier* declared that to advocate secularism was to betray Lebanon. He meant that the preservation of the status quo depended upon providing Christians with the necessary guarantees and, by implication, with the necessary political power.

The Lebanese idea, and the quest to give this idea aesthetic expression, was manifest in the days of the French mandate, when many Christians, even if they finally became restive under direct French rule, believed that Lebanon was in fact now independent and that it was theirs. This was the case with many of the writers in the *Revue Phénicienne*, for example, founded in 1920 by Charles Corm, one of the leading writers of the day. The title of the journal itself suggests the identification of Lebanon with its Phoenician heritage, and poets writing in it—Elie Tyan, Hector Klat (a Greek Orthodox), and Corm himself, among others—would play upon the theme that both French and Arabic have somehow been transformed in Lebanon to replace Phoenician, the regretted lost language of the ancestors, as the vehicle of expression of the Phoenician genius. Frequent symbols and refrains in the poetry of the 1920s through the 1940s included the Mountain—Corm's most famous work was a three-part epic entitled *La montagne inspirée* [The magical mountain] (1934)—the desert, and the sea; Cadmus; Europa; the alphabet (bestowed by the Phoenicians upon civilization); the village with its warmth and simplicity, as opposed to the decadent city; and the French language, of whose "douceurs tyranniques" (tyrannical sweetness) Hector Klat wrote and through which he could express his "Phoenician" and "oriental" soul. And it was with bittersweet ambivalence that Farjallah Haik, another Christian Lebanese poet, attacked the last of the French mandate in his *Dieu est libanais* [God is Lebanese] (1945) and indicated that Lebanon wanted French culture, but not French overlords.

These writers, and their contemporary successors, were deeply influenced by French literature, the romantics and the symbolists in particular, as were those who wrote in Arabic. Among writers in Arabic who have influenced the development of modern free verse techniques in poetry and who have helped to produce a simpler, more direct prose style have been Lebanese Christians as well as Muslims. Among the outstanding contemporary poets are Khalil Hawi, a Greek Orthodox, and Adonis, a Shi'ite Muslim. Also important have been an earlier group of émigré writers in the United States, the best known of whom is Gibran Kahlil Gibran, who wrote in both Arabic and English.

All these writers have owed a great deal to the inspiration of Western writers and poets, including T. S. Eliot, Rimbaud, and Valéry, and to the translation into Arabic of many of their works. In this enterprise of translating the best of the West, Lebanon has played a major role, second only to that of Egypt. Suleiman Bustani, the brother of Butrus, published his translation of *The Iliad* into Arabic as early as 1903, and more recently, the novelist Suhail Idris has translated works of Camus and Sartre.

Since independence, the tendency has been for poets, both in Arabic and French, to explore more universal rather than regionalist themes and to experiment with new techniques. The same has been true of painters. Among those who write in French, Georges Shehadeh, the most outstanding Lebanese dramatist, might be recognized as Lebanese only because of his name.

For literature written in Arabic, the trimestrial review *Sh'ir* [Poetry], a leading vehicle for the "modernists," which was founded in 1957 by the Christian poet Yusuf al-Khal, has been of great importance. Inevitably, because Arabic as a language is so intertwined with a particular tradition and religion, the "ancients" have regarded the experiments with language of the "moderns," and their revolt against traditional verse forms and prescriptions, with indignation, even arguing on occasion that the modernists do not know Arabic! This battle of generations and of traditions is of great moment in a culture that esteems "the word" so highly and in which poets are objects of particular veneration.

Conservatives are also indignant at efforts by some Lebanese intellectuals and scholars to try to standardize and to "modernize" the very difficult diglossic language (i.e., a language with marked differences between the spoken and the written) that Arabic is, both to improve the ease of discourse on modern subjects and to provide a more consistent vocabulary for the sciences. Many Arabs have participated in this effort; two Lebanese in the forefront have been Anis Frayha and Abdullah al-'Alayla (a Muslim). The latter has worked on a dictionary along Western lines, for example, one that lists words as they occur in discourse rather than, as is traditional, by roots, a system that often involves confusion and a considerable expenditure of time.

Among the themes of the more contemporary poets have been those of existentialist anguish (*qalaq*) over personal and national identity and over the stultifying hold of tradition on creativity and individual freedom. Some poets have regarded themselves as *poètes maudits*, sometimes with defiance and self-indulgence. Other themes have been those of humiliation, national as well as personal, and the emptiness and boredom of the crassly materialistic modern Arab city.

This anxiety, underlying so much of the contemporary poetry of Lebanon, has been common to the ethos in the Arab world as well as to much of the rest of the world. Some of the anxiety has been the product of circumstances particular to the Arab world—the creation of Israel and the Palestinian diaspora, for example, or the humiliating defeat at the hands of Israel in 1967. And some of this anguish has been rooted in the Lebanese experience itself. Particular to the latter might be perceptions by writers and intellectuals of the governing "establishment" as selfish, self-seeking, immobilist, and incapable of changing a system that cries for reform or of committing itself and the nation to specific causes. The confessional structure of Lebanon has also been a source of anguish, because it has been perceived by many as forcing the individual, through community pressures, to be identified and to identify himself with his own sect and so to be boxed in and denied the chance of being judged, and of being able to respond, in terms of purely human and universal norms. Confessionalism also, the complaint has been, is an important guarantee that life in Lebanon can never transcend mediocrity because social roles are determined by sect and by influence, not by merit.

Related to this, and a source of much negativism and cynicism as well as dilettantism, has been the overwhelming preoccupation, in this hothouse of intrigue and factionalism, with politics to the exclusion of other endeavors of greater and universal significance. Particularly frustrating for many has been the atmosphere of suspiciousness and distrust of foreigners as well as of compatriots engendered by the small size and the regional vulnerability of Lebanon. Even Charles Malik, the eminent teacher and statesman who has been seen by friend and foe alike as one of the leading spokesmen of Lebanon's special identity, on the eve of the collapse of 1975 spoke of the sterile "Phoenician commercialism" and the "levantinism" in Lebanon and warned of the danger that, as the soul is lost in cosmopolitanism, there is a potential for mindless and destructive violence.

Some of Lebanon's leading newspaper columnists have also been highly critical of the Lebanese system. These critics include figures of considerable importance on the Beirut scene, among them Ghassan Toueni, Rushdi Ma'luf, George Naccache, and René Aggiouri. Frequently they could write with despair or with wit about Lebanon. Aggiouri, in *L'Orient–Le Jour*, might question whether Lebanon had ever been a nation at all; Ma'luf in his Arabic column "Useful Bits of Information" (Mukhtasar Mufid) once suggested, with humor, that Lebanon was well on its way to becoming a nation, that it was halfway there already: "Nations of the world enact laws, and they execute them; our country enacts laws. . . . Nations of the world demand respect and they enforce this respect. Our nation demands respect." Toueni, in *Al-Nahar*, once suggested that the Lebanese live behind masks; they say one thing publicly and another thing privately. Naccache, in *L'Orient*, after listing the fractious and anarchic traits of his countrymen, could add with bemused confidence, echoing Galileo, "nevertheless it moves."

A recent theme among some Muslim intellectuals and ideologues, Adonis for one, partly in response to the Iranian revolution and out of disgust with the West, has been what is sometimes referred to as the "Muslim option." The thesis has been that Western ideologies have proved bankrupt and that Arabs should now cultivate a Muslim sensibility and remodel their institutions in line with those of the Islamic past. How deep or permanent this tendency will prove remains to be seen;

one might only suggest that it is hardly congruent with the Lebanese idea. Among Muslim intellectuals who oppose this tendency has been Sadiq al-Azm, to whom it appears regressive and reactionary. Is al-Azm only a maverick?

It is evident from this brief summary of intellectual and artistic life in contemporary Lebanon that the schism in the heart of Lebanon has been more than political or institutional; it has run deep in the psyche and the soul. This schism has found a reflection in the Lebanese systems of education and is perpetuated through these.

EDUCATION

Many of the problems inherent in Lebanese society have been reflected in the educational system. The most important of these was the schizophrenic dichotomy running through the republic's very essence. Halim Barakat in his *Lebanon in Strife* (1977) indicated that on the eve of 1975, most Christian university students were hostile to the Palestinians, saw themselves as either reformist or conservative, and were loyal to Lebanon. Most Muslim university students, on the other hand, saw themselves as pro-Palestinian, progressive, and Pan-Arabist. Significantly, the poorer the student, the more radical, the more pro-Palestinian, and the more alienated from his family he was likely to be. But, equally significant, the majority across the board felt greater identification with family and sect than with class.

Public education has been inferior in quality to private education. Many parents skimped to send their children to private school. In 1964, 42 percent of primary and secondary school children attended public school; in 1970, 84 percent of the primary schools were nongovernmental Only 13 percent of the national budget was devoted to public education in the 1950s (compared to 20 to 25 percent in Tunisia, Iraq, and Algeria only in 1971 did the figure rise to 20 percent. Almost none of th public school teachers have had any training; the Lebanese Universi had only seven full-time teachers in the 1960s; government encou agement of scientific research (a check to the brain drain) was nonexiste until 1963, when the National Research Council was established (w only 1 percent of the national budget).

The Christian establishment has consistently supported priv education and defended it from inroads by public education or f any serious constraints. Article 10 of the Constitution guarantees and so private, education, and efforts to control and supervise curr have been half-hearted and usually ineffective. The establishme the Educational Center for Research and Development in 1972 had

chance to discipline the educational Proteus, with its multiplicity of diverse systems, standards, and languages, before the collapse of 1975.

Except for the need to know Arabic well enough to pass the baccalaureate, the key to university status and to government employment, schools were by and large left to their own devices. The result has been to deepen the ideological cleavages between the various communities and between the two Lebanons, as can be seen in regard to two important bearers of cultural and ideological orientation, history and language, where education's "political socialization" function, to work toward a national consensus, has been a failure in the main.

History, from elementary through secondary school, has been taught either to promote the Phoenician concept of Lebanon's past, with an emphasis upon Rome and France along the way and upon specifically Lebanese heroes such as Fakhr al-Din or Bashir II, or to emphasize Lebanon's Arab heritage, with an emphasis upon the great Umayyad and Abbasid pasts and upon heroes ranging from Saladin to Nasser. The first conception of the past has served to distinguish Lebanon from the Arab world and has emphasized links with the West (the Phoenicians brought the alphabet to the West and, through the legend of Europa and Zeus, gave Europe its name); to many Muslims this conception has only served to isolate Lebanon from the Arab and Muslim world and to provide a base for Western imperialist intrusions into the area, be it by the Crusaders or U.S. Marines. The second conception has tended to deny Lebanon its specificity (as a haven for minorities, as a bridge between the West and the East), and to many Christians this denial has constituted a threat to Lebanon's sovereignty.

One might recommend, if the dichotomy is ever to be overcome in the interest of unity, the approach advocated by perceptive historians such as Kamal Salibi as an alternative option. Salibi's contention has been that Lebanon does have a specific character, one that is threatening neither to Christian nor to Muslim susceptibilities. This specificity is rooted not in any Phoenician past (this, Salibi maintains, is unhistorical) or exclusively in the Arab heritage, although this is an important ingredient, but in the experiment and in the experience of cooperation and symbiosis between sects that began in the seventeenth century under the Druze amirs. Lebanon, the argument is, should be seen as an accomplishment in multiethnic living, one that when passions have remained cool and toleration has been practiced, has produced, in spite of religious variegation, prosperity and benefit not only to the Lebanese, but to the Arab world in general. By adopting such an approach in textbooks one might someday provide Lebanese students with a common source of pride and of patriotism. But sadly, the prospects for such an approach have tended to be dim.

As for language, it is not strange that patriotic Lebanese intellectuals such as Sélim Abou should insist that, unlike in other Arab countries, French is as much a Lebanese language as is Arabic. Nor is it strange that many Western-educated Lebanese should still hold to the cliché that French is Lebanon's language of culture, English its language of commerce, and Arabic the language of daily intercourse and administration or to the other cliché that while French (and English) are languages of modernity, Arabic is a language of dreams and rhetoric, devoid of the structure or the common vocabulary needed to serve as a useful tool in science and technology. To most Muslims, of course, such clichés smack of what Edward Said has called "Orientalism"—the tendency of Western scholars to reify and to disparage Eastern cultures; they are insults to the sacred language of Islam; they ignore the fact that in the Middle Ages, Arabic was for a period the language of science and philosophy for the whole educated Mediterranean world; and, of course, they militate against an essential bond of the "Arab nation," classical Arabic.

So strongly do many Christian Lebanese feel about their French identification that any challenge to the French linguistic and cultural presence is seen as a threat. In early 1972, for example, cries of alarm were heard when President Franjiyya appointed a cabinet of "experts," a plurality of whom were graduates of the American University of Beirut (A.U.B.), and when the first director of the Educational Center for Research and Development was also a graduate and faculty member at the A.U.B. French *is*, in fact, an important national dimension for many Christian Lebanese, and eminent Muslim leaders such as Abdallah Yafi and Sa'b Salam have sent their children to French private schools. In 1975, eighty-five French language schools taught 55,940 students. Some of Lebanon's important writers have written their works in French, and among important cultural institutions have been the Centre d'Etudes Supérieures, the Institut d'Archéologie, and St. Joseph, the training ground for many Lebanese lawyers and political leaders.

The issue of whether bilingualism, or trilingualism, in education is harmful has often been debated in the media. One position has been that education in more than one language frustrates the child's mental development and sense of identity and has tended to produce a cosmopolitan mentality dangerous to the nation; the other position has been that multilingualism is a valuable cultural asset and a necessity for a merchant-republic, as well as a guarantor of Lebanon's specificity. The debate is likely to continue so long as there is a Lebanon, but one could argue that if other problems are ever solved and common principles are accepted, Lebanon could live with multilingualism, as have other nations with a common sense of identity—Tunisia, for example, or

52

SOCIETY

TABLE 3.2   Education

	Number of Schools	Number of Pupils	Number of Teachers
Public Schools			
Primary	740	202,913	
Upper primary	549	77,161	{17,077
Secondary	65	18,240	
Private Schools			
Primary & Kindergarten	742	{366,987	{16,168
Upper primary & secondary	390		
Universities			
American University at Beirut (English)[a]		4,600	500
Beirut Arab University (Arabic)		27,000	180
Lebanese University (Arabic)		14,826	733
Saint Joseph (French)		5,663	479
University of Kaslik (Arabic)		510	230

[a]Predominant language of instruction given in parentheses.

Notes: In 1978, there were 50,803 students (45.7% of them Lebanese) at 12 institutions of higher education, including the 5 universities listed in the table. Other institutions are the French Centre d'Etudes Supérieures, Beirut University College (for women) and Hagazian, an Armenian college (English has been the predominant language of the last two). There are also several technical schools: the National School of Arts and Crafts; two agricultural schools with three-year programs; the Higher Teachers' College (at the Lebanese University; and several lower-level public schools.

Switzerland. In Lebanon's case, however, where language is so symbolic and feelings about it so visceral, the only hope might be to adopt Arabic as the base language of education, with other languages taught in later years as second languages. But this, again, is a chicken-and-egg proposition; it assumes a consensus that multilingualism has served to preclude.

    Another social factor that has had important consequences for Lebanon has been the "educational explosion" since independence, a phenomenon common to many newly independent nations. As an increasing number of students receive their degrees, and with them expectations of a better status and income in life, a dangerous situation arises if the economy is unable to provide sufficient outlets for employment. This was increasingly so in Lebanon. The result has been alienation from the system and an increasing radicalization within the student body, one naturally exploited by the various political parties. Between 1959 and 1963 the number of public schools quadrupled, and by the end of the 1960s Lebanon could take pride in having added to its universities the national Lebanese University, the Beirut Arab University, and the University of Kaslik. In 1950 there were 115 students in primary school per 1,000 inhabitants; in 1963 the figure was 160. In 1959 there were 6,822 university students; by 1963 the number had grown to 15,978. It is not strange that after 1967 student radicalism and student action should have become an important factor for destabilization. In the 1970s there were an increasing number of demonstrations, clashes between students and the security forces, and campus battles between radical and conservative students. Often these clashes took place in the streets as well as on campuses.

The most troublesome to the government were the students of the Lebanese University, swollen by 1975 to some 10,000 students. In 1970 the university had a forty-day strike; in March 1972 the premises of the Ministry of Education were invaded; in April 1973 there was a march upon Parliament. Demands voiced included reductions in fees, increases in student subsidies, the abolition of reforms designed to raise academic requirements for graduation, and the improvement of educational facilities; but political motives were almost always implicit, if not explicit. When students threw stones and the security forces would charge, for example, the retreating students might shout at them, "Cowards, instead of brutalizing your own sons why don't you go south to defend Lebanon against Israel!" Frequently establishment personalities were denounced by name. The tumultuous activities of the students may have been in part psychodrama and cases of frustrated and pent-up adolescent energy, but they anticipated, as Halim Barakat has observed, the breakdown of 1975.[9]

Usually, student demands would be opposed by conservative elements such as the Kata'ib and supported by the left. While the former would, for example, denounce the recognition of Syrian and Egyptian degrees as equivalent to Lebanon's as a threat to academic standards, the latter would interpret the effort to abolish this equivalence as a threat to Arabism and as a case of cultural imperialism. Another case in which this dichotomy was revealed was the long dispute (1960–1962) over whether the newly founded Arab University of Beirut, with its affiliation with Egypt, should be allowed to issue law degrees. A long strike by Lebanese lawyers, one motivated in part by professional exclusiveness and in party by the objection to foreign intrusion into Lebanon's affairs, was ended only when it was agreed that although the degrees could be issued, foreign law programs would come under strict government supervision.

After 1975, enrollment in Lebanon's major universities rose, surprisingly, from 45,000 in 1975 to 55,000 in 1978. One reason for this was easier access when these universities established new branches in various parts of Lebanon (because transit across parts of Beirut and elsewhere was difficult or dangerous). In addition, St. Joseph, eager to increase the number of its Muslim students, set up branches in Tripoli and Sidon and raised its enrollment from 4,000 in 1975 to some 5,600 in 1978. The Lebanese University became fully decentralized, with sixteen branches and more than 14,000 students in 1978. The American University of Beirut in 1976 opened a branch in Christian Ashrafiyya, with 300 students in 1978; while the A.U.B.'s enrollment fell during the Civil War it rose to the prewar figure of 4,000 to 5,000 by 1978. The Arab University of Beirut, serving mainly Palestinian students, had some 27,000 students in 1982. The expanding University of the Holy Spirit (see Chapter 6) had more than 500 students in 1978.

Each of these universities, as one might expect, has had its own particularity and its own reputation, as well as its own role in the cultural life of Lebanon. St. Joseph, for example, which has traditionally educated much of the Christian elite, has served mainly to educate Lebanese students; the A.U.B., on the other hand, has educated students from the whole Middle Eastern area and beyond. And it has had a reputation as a breeding ground for dangerous radicalism in spite of the fact that along with a George Habash, it has also educated an arch-conservative like Charles Malik. A random sampling of leading establishment personalities alive in 1979 shows that of some twenty, ten had studied at the A.U.B. and ten at St. Joseph.

The entire educational system in its variegation has reinforced the pluralism of the society and like most other spheres of Lebanese life, unfortunately, has been marked by communal and regional disparities. On the sectarian totem pole, the best educated are the Christians, with a literacy rate twice that of the Muslims (with the Maronites the most literate among the Christians). The Druzes have been next, slightly above the Sunnites; the Shi'ites have been at the bottom. In 1962 illiteracy rates among Christians were 23 percent for men, 45 percent for women; among Muslims the figures were 39 percent for men, 69 percent for women. Most Christians have gone to the better-staffed and -equipped private schools (foreign and Lebanese); most Muslim youths have attended the poorly financed public schools.

Such disparities between class, sect, and region have not augured well for the nation in spite of the countervailing forces apologists have pointed to: Primordial loyalties have been stronger than class loyalties, the poorest Lebanese has been better off than his counterpart in other Arab countries, and even the Shi'ites have been increasing their representation in administration and in the police force. One could argue, of course, that other societies have responded effectively to challenges of gross social disparity. The question confronting Lebanon was whether it was institutionally equipped to meet such challenges without jeopardizing the delicate balances upon which the nation rested.

NOTES

1. Paul Starr, "Ethnic Categories and Identifications in Lebanon: A Descriptive Investigation," *Urban Life*, April 1978, pp. 111–142.

2. Yusif Sayigh, *Entrepreneurs of Lebanon: The Role of the Business Leader in a Developing Economy* (Cambridge, Mass.: Harvard University Press, 1962), p. 69.

3. Samih K. Farsoun, "Family Structure and Society in Modern Lebanon," in Louise E. Sweet, ed., *Peoples and Cultures of the Middle East: Volume II: Life in Cities, Towns and Countryside* (New York: Natural History Press, 1970), pp. 257–307.

4. E. T. Prothro and Lutfy Diab, *Changing Family Patterns in the Arab East* (Beirut: American University of Beirut, 1974).

5. James A. Bill and Carl Leiden, *Politics in the Middle East* (Boston: Little, Brown and Co., 1979), p. 21.

6. Fuad L. Khuri, "The Changing Class Structure in Lebanon," *Middle East Journal*, Winter 1969, pp. 29–44.

7. Kamal Joumblatt, *Pour le Liban* [In behalf of Lebanon] (Paris: Stock, 1978), p. 127.

8. Samir Khalaf and Per Kongstad, *Hamra of Beirut: A Case of Rapid Modernization* (London: E. J. Brill, 1973).

9. Halim Barakat, *Lebanon in Strife: Student Preludes to the Civil War* (Austin: University of Texas Press, 1977).

4

Economy

Lebanon's has been one of the few pure models of a laissez-faire economy in the modern world. A foreign consultant, once asked how to improve the economy, said he didn't know, but to leave it alone. And it was because of its dynamic private sector that on the eve of political suicide Lebanon was prosperous.

ACCOMPLISHMENTS

Between 1950 and 1963, per capita income rose from $235 to $449 and the gross national product (GNP) from $520 million to $735 million; foreign holdings rose from $86.5 million in 1955 to $236 million in 1965; the money supply rose from $80 million in 1954 to $180 million in 1964; between 1964 and 1969 the annual rate of growth was 7 percent and, with a population increase of 2 percent per annum, per capita income rose by 5 percent; and the number of U.S. companies increased from 147 to 264 between 1961 and 1965, a clear sign of confidence in the economy.

These accomplishments were due largely to ability, a favorable geographical location, and entrepreneurship. With virtually no mineral resources, Lebanon produces little more than fruits, vegetables, cotton, tobacco, olive oil, some cereals, cattle, and illegal hashish. Imports in 1960 ($380 million) far exceeded exports ($70 million). The deficit was made up comfortably, however, by invisible earnings from tourism, transit trade, and other services, remittances from Lebanese abroad, and revenues from oil terminals. (During much of the Civil War and its aftermath the refineries did not operate. The Tripoli refinery, for example, resumed operations only in 1981.) Only about 12 percent of GNP was produced by small industry and only 18 percent by agriculture, which accounted for a third of GNP; while overall growth was 7 percent a year, industry and agriculture were growing by only 5 percent and 3.6 percent respectively.

Produce arrives on the outskirts of Beirut. (Credit: *Middle East Insight*)

Among the unusual innovators, most of whom were Christians, was Emile Bustani, a very successful contractor who became a deputy (and upon his tragic death in his private plane in 1961 was succeeded by his daughter Myrna). His was a case of a person who, purely on the basis of ability and wealth, entered the establishment. He became a leading adviser to President Chamoun (in local parlance, his "sultan," i.e., *éminence grise*) and married into the prestigious Khazins, once a great feudal family. He might have become a candidate for the presidency. His Contracting and Trading Company (CAT) did business throughout the Arab world.

Another leading entrepreneur was Munir Abu Haydar, who turned a small air-freight service, which had only one four-engine York in 1965, into the largest all-cargo airline in the Middle East, Trans-Mediterranean Airways (TMA). TMA used Boeing 707s to transport, among many other articles, chicken foods from Britain to Japan and car components to Bahrain. Albert and Edwin Abela, who started their careers during World War II as caterers to the British army, by 1971 had built what has been called the largest catering service in the world, providing hot meals, for example, to thirty different nations. The company's turnover was more than $70 million. And the privately owned Middle East Airlines (MEA), organized by Najib Alamuddin,

TABLE 4.1   Trade: Imports and Exports by Country, 1975
(in percentages)

	Imports into Lebanon	Exports from Lebanon
Saudi Arabia	n.a.	14.9
Syria	9.0	12.0
Jordan	1.0	8.6
Kuwait	n.a.	6.8
Iraq	2.7	6.0
U.S.A.	13.2	5.9
U.K.	18.6	4.5
France	9.2	3.7
Italy	5.8	3.7
Egypt	1.3	2.9
USSR	n.a.	2.7
W. Germany	7.5	2.4

Source: The Middle East and North Africa, 1979-80, 26th
ed. (London: Europa Publications, 1979).

was generally considered to be the most efficiently run airline in the
Arab world, perhaps in the Third World. Its home base, Beirut's
International Airport, opened in 1951, was imaginatively designed for
jet airplanes before these were used commercially. MEA was Lebanon's
largest employer in 1975 (some 5,600).

An indication of Lebanese resilience is that MEA, although it lost
LL 69.1 million (the exchange rate normally varies from three to four
Lebanese pounds to the dollar, although in August 1982 it fell as low
as five to the dollar) during the Civil War, in 1979 made plans to
purchase nineteen new planes over a seven-year period, to the tune of
$150 million. In 1981, even with a $15.82 million loss (through July)
Salim Salam, managing director, talked of expansion. The Israeli invasion
of 1982 and the closure of the airport of course deferred such projections
temporarily.

Trade is of crucial importance in Lebanon's economy. The major
imports are precious metals, stones, and coins; transport equipment;
industrial raw materials; and cars (in 1974, 41,124 cars were registered).
The most important exports are building materials (41 percent of total
exports) and food and agricultural goods (26 percent). In 1978 half of
Lebanon's imports came from Italy (LL 714 million), France (LL 574
million), the United States (LL 379 million), West Germany (LL 376
million), and the United Kingdom (LL 347 million). The largest markets
for Lebanon were Arab countries (85–87 percent); the largest single
market was Saudi Arabia (40 percent). Thus Lebanon, overall, imports

TABLE 4.2 Value of Imports and Exports by Country, 1973
(LL '000)

Imports (only major exporters shown)		Exports and Re-Exports (only largest clients shown)	
France	361,915	France	161,912
West Germany	380,839	Kuwait	105,497
Italy	293,724	Saudi Arabia	260,910
Japan	126,233	United Kingdom	148,288
Switzerland	141,886	United States	72,069
United Kingdom	261,409	Iraq	50,075
United States	377,542	Jordan	51,020
Iraq	119,919	Syria	77,403

Source: The Middle East and North Africa, 1979-80, 26th
ed. (London: Europa Publications, 1979).

TABLE 4.3 Imports and Exports, 1973 (in LL '000)

Imports

Precious stones, jewelry, coins	640,237
Vegetable products	292,868
Machinery and electrical apparatus	479,325
Textiles and products	413,261
Non-precious metals and products	346,365
Transport vehicles	322,734
Animals and animal products	131,140
Industrial chemical products	259,480
Mineral products	187,469
Beverages and tobacco	150,428

Exports and Re-Exports

Vegetable products	145,354
Precious metals, stones, jewelry, coins	333,989
Animals and animal products	51,874
Machinery and electrical apparatus	168,238
Non-previous metals and products	114,037
Textiles and products	172,662
Beverages and tobacco	87,559
Transport vehicles	150,162

Source: Adapted from The Middle East and North
Africa, 1979-80, 26th ed. (London: Europa Publications, 1979).

from the West and exports to the rest of the Arab world. In 1965 and then in 1977 Lebanon negotiated with the European Economic Community to lower tariffs on its goods and, in the latter year, to obtain low-interest loans and grants of $33 million from the European Investment Bank.

As already noted, invisible earnings have been very important in covering Lebanon's trade deficit, which quadrupled from LL 260 million to LL 1,138 million between 1951 and 1966. Total external earnings (LL 1,883.4 million in 1966) easily covered this deficit. In 1966 merchandise exports produced only LL 584.1 million, while services (foreign travel, transportation, insurance, investment income, government, transit services, etc.) produced LL 1,164.8 million, a ratio of one to two. Trade activity in general and banking, insurance, and exchange transactions produce one-third of the national income. Also important as a source of revenue have been capital movements (producing LL 15.4 million in 1965) and émigré remittances, which, together with foreign aid, charitable donations, and such, produced LL 6.4 million in 1965.

In 1973 it was evident that patterns of the 1960s were continuing. At this time estimated imports were LL 4,066 million, and exports were LL 2,542. The GNP at this time was $3 billion. In 1979, the balance of payments surplus was $200 million.

Another source of income has been tourism. By 1965 Lebanon already had 320 hotels to serve some 179,000 visitors (50 percent of them from Arab countries). In 1974 the total number of visitors (excluding Syrians) was 1,510,260. This figure included 892,203 from Arab countries, 316,080 from European countries, and 143,000 from the Americas. Tourism produced about 20 percent of GNP before the Civil War.

Transportation facilities included the airport, which served 2,806,628 passengers in 1974, and the port, at which 3,972 ships called in that year and which handled 5,057,545 metric tons of cargo. In 1973 Lebanon's railroads made 36,000 journeys, handling 2,829,000 passengers and 512,000 metric tons of goods. Passenger service provided LL 81,000, transport of goods, LL 2,446,000. Lebanon has 4,400 miles (7,100 kilometers) of roads (1,194 miles, or 1,990 kilometers, are main roads); 208 miles (335 kilometers) of standard-gauge tracks; and 56 miles (90 kilometers) of narrow-gauge tracks. In 1974 it had 220,204 cars and taxis, 2,397 buses, 20,983 trucks, and 13,179 motocycles. In 1974, 2,613 ships (5,276,000 tonnage) visited the harbor; 3,411,546 metric tons entered the port and 667,841 metric tons were cleared. The airport in this same year was used by 44,406 airplanes and 2,807,000 passengers; through it passed 145,897 metric tons of goods.

Beirut, before the unraveling of the society in 1975, was regional home and headquarters to companies from all over the world. It provided banking and transit facilities to the increasingly oil-wealthy Middle East; it could offer educated and capable office personnel with an easy knowledge of needed languages; its infrastructure worked; crime in the streets was minimal; it had good schools for foreign children; and it could afford almost any pleasure for their parents.

VULNERABILITY

But although its performance was impressive, Lebanon's economy was beset by many problems, and it was unusually vulnerable to outside pressures. While, as a haven, it could draw on a pool of talented "creative minorities" (in Joseph Schumpeter's phrase), like other Third World countries it suffered from brain drain. The college graduates, for example, who emigrated between 1962 and 1966 to the United States and Canada included 35 percent of Lebanon's engineers, 10.5 percent of its biologists, 9.3 percent of its doctors, and 18 percent of its sociologists.[1] One reason for this exodus was the rapidity with which urbanization was outstripping industrialization at the same time that the "education explosion" was producing more graduates than the economy could employ. With its relatively high population density Lebanon was, in this respect, overpopulated.

Investment in industry rose 15 percent between 1960 and 1964, but between 1950 and 1968 it continued to constitute only about 12 percent of GNP, suggesting relative stagnation. A serious hurdle to industrial development has been the power of the merchant class, always hostile to any special treatment or protection for industry. In 1971, for example, proposals to raise duties on the import of luxury goods were quickly dropped when the Lebanese Merchants Association made clear its determined opposition. To this extent, Lebanon remained a comprador economy.

Another factor limiting industrial growth has been the unequal distribution of income; this has weakened domestic demand as a stimulus and discouraged the formation of larger establishments. Lebanese industry has been small-scale. The average number of workers per plant rose only to twenty-one from eighteen between 1955 and 1964. In 1964, 51 percent of all establishments employed fewer than ten people; 85 percent fewer than twenty-five, and 94 percent fewer than fifty. And these figures are on the optimistic side, as they exclude many small plants employing fewer than five persons.

More recently industrial production did rise, but only to provide 16 percent of GNP (LL 1,040 million in 1973–1974). At this time industry employed 120,000 persons. In 1973 the number of limited liability companies was eighteen; by 1974 it had risen to forty-four. Since the

Civil War, revenues from industry—perhaps LL 1,000 million in 1978—
have been impressive, but only if one ignored the factor of inflation.
The largest employers, apart from the oil companies, have been food
processing and textiles. Over the years the government and the foreign
oil companies have haggled over fees for the use of the oil terminals
at Zahrani, near Sidon (for Saudi Arabian oil) and Tripoli (for Iraqi oil
through Syria). Each time the government has managed to increase
these fees. In 1962, for example, Tapline, a branch of ARAMCO, agreed
to increase them to $4.5 million and to pay $12.5 million for past fees.
It is believed by some that Lebanon may have oil, particularly offshore,
and in 1975 bids were received by various companies to explore. But
events have prevented any progress to date.

After the Civil War, the government attempted to encourage
industrial development with low-interest loans and by providing foreign
companies with damage insurance, including coverage of losses in civil
war, through the National Establishment for Investment Insurance.

To 1982, agriculture, which employed some 60 percent of the
population, produced only one-fifth of the GNP. Lebanon had a food
surplus in citrus fruits and apples; the only rapidly expanding sector
was poultry. Wheat had to be imported. Of the 400,000 cultivable
hectares (1 million acres—40 percent of the total land surface), 17
percent lay fallow each year and was used for seasonal pasturage.
Between 1948 and 1966 the amount of cultivable land increased by 3
percent per annum and between 1950 and 1960 revenues from agriculture
rose from LL 206 million to LL 380 million. These developments were
partly the result of increasing irrigation through river projects, particularly
on the Litani River in the south; the better utilization of fertilizers
encouraged by the Green Plan (discussed in the next section); and the
work of the School of Agriculture of the American University of Beirut
and its experimental farm in the Biqa' Valley.

Large landholdings and sharecropping (18 percent of the land)
have been a feature of the outlying areas only, the south in particular,
where some 20 percent of the population has owned about 50 percent
of the land. *In toto*, plots of more than 40 hectares (100 acres) have
been owned by 18 percent of the landowners and plots of 20–40 hectares
(50–100 acres) by 17 percent of the population; the rest have been
owned in plots of 5 hectares (12.5 acres) or less. Inheritance laws
providing for equal sharing of an estate by the heirs—in an extreme
case a farmer might inherit only one branch of a tree!—contribute to
the large number of small plots.

One of the chief weaknesses of this economy, so dependent on
invisible earnings, has been its vulnerability to the vagaries of fortune.
Joseph Malone has suggested that the Casino du Liban, the luxurious

TABLE 4.4   Industry

	Number of Plants	Percentage of Total Labor Force
Industries (1964)		
Food products	491	2.9
Beverages	43	
Textiles	121	2
Footwear and clothing	274	1.2
Wood industry	82	0.3
Furniture	230	
Paper and paper products	36	
Printing & allied industries	185	0.5
Leather	154	0.3
Rubber products	14	0.2
Chemical products	54	0.2
Nonmetallic products	309	1.4
Metal products	137	1.2
Transportation & electrical products	21	
Miscellaneous	47	

	Output (metric tons)
Industries (1974)	
Petrol	814,000
Kerosene	229,000
Gas oil	4,207,000
Fuel oil	9,107,000
Butane	631,000
Tobacco manufacturing	6,337
Cement	1,744,000
Timber	54,451 (cubic meters)
Electricity	1,975 (million kilowatts)

Source: The Middle East and North Africa, 1979-80, 26th ed. (London: Europa Publications, 1979).

gambling establishment north of Beirut, might be taken as the symbol of the risk by which the Lebanese lived.[2] In financial circles, gossip often included speculation as to the meaning of any increase or decrease of cash flow into the country; a considerable and sudden increase might, for example, be held to indicate that foreign powers intended some sort of a political coup or that an election was considered to be of some importance.

Ever since 1950, when Syria, having adopted a *dirigiste* approach to its economy, ended the customs union with Lebanon, political leverage had on occasion been exerted by closing the border to Lebanon's transit goods to other parts of the Arab world. And in 1965–1966, the flourishing

TABLE 4.5   Agriculture

	Hectares harvested (1975) ('000)	Production (thousand metric tons)
Wheat	75	79
Barley	7	5
Sugar beets	3	145
Potatoes	9	80
Onions	2	31
Tobacco	8	10
Citrus fruits	--	284
Apples	--	170
Grapes	17	100
Olives	--	35
Tomatoes	5	60

Livestock ('000)

Goats	330
Sheep	232
Cattle	84
Donkeys	22
Chickens	7,074

Source: The Middle East and North Africa, 1979-80, 26th ed. (London: Europa Publications, 1979).

Intra Bank, which was run by the Palestinian Yusuf Beidas and was the pride of many Palestinians, crashed when Kuwait, the USSR, and Saudi Arabia, each for its own reasons, all withdrew their deposits at the same time. One side effect, parenthetically, of this crash, and the failure of the Lebanese banks to offer a helping hand, was to increase Palestinian hostility to their Lebanese host.

Economists such as Nadim Khalaf have long warned that because industrial production and exports are relatively so low, and because of Lebanon's extraordinary propensity to import and to cover its deficits from services and invisible earnings, the nation has been subject to foreign pressures and manipulation. In particular, Khalaf has pointed to the operation of a sort of vicious circle: Success and prosperity in the services sector has attracted much Lebanese initiative away from more productive and stabilizing sectors and bred a "service" and mercantile mentality, which, in turn, discourages development in these other sectors.[3]

Another potential threat to the economy has been that political changes in other parts of the world would cut off the flow of remittances and that migration as a safety valve might end. This, in fact, did occur in certain African countries after they attained their independence. After 1975, as Beirut became increasingly unattractive as a center for foreign financial and commercial activity and offices were moved elsewhere, there was the danger for the future that countries such as Kuwait and Bahrain would develop facilities in competition with those of Lebanon. Beirut was already facing competition, before the Civil War, from rival ports such as Latakia and Aqaba as these were expanded. A related danger has been that, increasingly, oil revenue deposits once invested through Beirut now go directly to Switzerland and elsewhere.

A final weakness of the Lebanese economic system has been the communal and regional disparities it exhibits. In the liberal professions and on an employer-manager level, 73 percent were non-Muslims in 1962. Among a sample of more than 200 entrepreneurs studied by Yusif Sayigh,[4] only one-sixth were Muslims. The annual per capita income in 1960 in Beirut was $803; in the south it was $151. The Mountain, with 29 percent of the population, had 38.2 percent of all schools; the south, with 19 percent of the population, had only 14.8 percent of the schools. Among the roughly forty villages in the predominantly Muslim Akkar (the far north) there was no doctor available for a population of about 200,000. The death rate in the "Belt of Poverty" around Beirut was two to three times the national average.

In 1959, when the average per capita income was $327, the income of those included in the categories of desperate and very poor was $147; in the wealthier sector, 0.44 percent of the work force produced 6 percent of GNP; and a person in the financial sector earned on the average forty-five times what a person in the agricultural sector earned. In the 1960s, when inflation became a serious problem and the cost of necessities (as well as education) rose, it was the poor and the middling who suffered. Between 1961 and 1964 salaries increased 47 percent, the cost of living 95 percent. An important source of this inflation, especially after 1973, when the price of oil quadrupled, was the oil money that flowed into the country, much of it invested ostentatiously in luxury villas and the like. As Michael Hudson put it, this wave of money induced "acute modernization" and increased social instability.[5]

Samih Farsoun has observed concerning the data in Table 4.6 that one should not regard with optimism the fact that the 32 percent who earn LL 2,500–5,000 are called "middling."[6] This sum ($1,600) is not an adequate salary for a sizable family. It is what a lower clerk or some skilled workers might make and possibly live alone on, but not more. It was in face of the challenge of such disparities, as well as of the other weaknesses of the laissez-faire economic and social system, that President Shihab and his entourage, after the crisis

TABLE 4.6   Economic Disparities by Income Group (1960
estimates)

Family Income Categories	Percentage of families	Average Income	% GNP Earned by Each Category
Very poor (<LL1,200)	8.8	1,000	1.8
Poor (1,200-2,500)	41.2	2,000	16.5
Middling (2,500-5,000)	32.0	3,500	22.4
Well-off (5,000-15,000)	14.0	10,000	28.0
Rich (>15,000)	4.0	40,000	32.0

Source: Based upon Institut de Recherches et de Formation
en vue de Développement (IRFED), Besoins et possibilités
du Liban (Beirut, 1960-1961).

TABLE 4.7   Economic Disparities by Economic Sectors (1957)

	Percentage of National Income	Percentage of Population Employed	National Income per Employed Person
Agriculture	16	49	LL 1,082
Industry	13	12	LL 3,500
Construction	3	7	LL 1,242
Transportation	5	5	LL 3,333
Commerce	31	12	LL 8,849
Finance	6	0.4	LL 45,500
Other services	10	11	LL 3,083
Government	7	4	LL 6,750

Source: Nadim Khalaf, Economic Implications of the Size
of Nations with Specific Reference to Lebanon (Leiden:
Brill, 1971).

of 1958, decided that Lebanon could no longer afford its usual self-
seeking and unbridled ways—even if, compared to other parts of the
Third World, the percentage of Lebanese below the poverty line was
one of the smallest.[7]

REFORM

The fresh approach to the economy now advocated—the *nahj al-
shihabi* (Shihab's way), or simply shihabism—in no way sought to
replace the dynamic private economy with a controlled economy; the
goal was rather to provide only broad controls and guidelines and to
attempt, through government action, to encourage a more equitable

distribution of wealth, to provide social services where these were absent, and to offer a modicum of social security to the underprivileged. On the whole, under Shihab and his successor, Charles Hilu, who supported the *nahj*, several important accomplishments were realized and a model was developed for the future, although no fundamental transformation of the Lebanese system occurred. In a sense, Suleiman Franjiyya's victory in 1970, and his defeat of his rival, Ilyas Sarkis, Shihab's chief of cabinet and protégé, marked the end of the *nahj*.

Even so, the effort was well worth the candle. Inspired by General de Gaulle, many would have it, Shihab sought to transcend ordinary politics, for which he expressed clear contempt, and to seek to create a basis for a positive consensus in the land through modernizing the administration of the state by replacing political patronage by expertise. Government investment in the public sector, which had been only 15 percent of the total budget before 1959, was doubled to 30 percent. The number of public employees increased by 1,700, mostly in the Ministries of Education and Public Works (and the army was raised from 10,000 to 15,000). With the advice of the French Jesuit economist Père Louis Lebret, a thorough study of Lebanon's economy was made under the Ministry of General Planning, and a five-year plan was prepared, to be financed to the tune of LL 5 billion, supported by a LL 300 million loan from Kuwait.

Supporting these forceful initiatives were the Kata'ib (at this time willing to experiment with reform), Rashid Karami, a number of other traditional Muslim leaders pleased by Shihab's friendliness to Egypt, and Kamal Joumblatt. Shihab's closest advisers, other than Sarkis and Lebret, were Jean Lay, a former French colonel described as the *éminence grise*, and top officers of the army with whom Shihab has spent much of his professional life as commander in chief.

How much was accomplished? On the positive side, the number of Muslims in the administrative structure was raised to parity with the Christians; welfare services to the aged and handicapped were extended under the newly established Office of Social Development; electricity and drinking water were provided to a number of remote villages; and the office of the Green Plan, established in 1963, was expanded to become probably the most impressive of Lebanon's public projects. Through this plan, loans were provided to poor farmers, and reforestation and canal drainage contributed to increasing agricultural productivity, however modestly. In addition, the activities of the National Litani Authority (established in 1954) were extended, and new dams and tunnels were built to generate more electricity. In 1964, one-seventh of Beirut's electric power came from the Litani—89,332,000 kilowatt hours—

and 40,000 hectares (100,000 acres) of cultivable land were added, through irrigation, to the deprived south.

Other agencies were established to help modernize the economy and the administration. In 1964 (when the authority to issue currency of the once French-owned Banque de Syrie et du Liban ended), the Central Bank was founded. A social security system, contributed to by both employer and employee, was inaugurated, to be administered through the Social Security Treasury (established by decree in 1963). According to this system, upon retirement a person receives a sum of money equivalent to one month's salary out of each year he has been employed. To date the system has worked out best for regular middle-class employees and worst for occasional and migrant workers.

To rationalize and improve administration, Shihab founded the Central Committee for Administrative Reform, the National Institute of Public Administration to train administrators, the Central Inspection Agency, and the Civil Service Council. It is little wonder that traditional leaders began to complain that they were being undermined politically, as sources of patronage were replaced by direct contact between government and people, and merchants began to fear that the "robber baron" days might be over. Not only did opposition increase, but it was also soon discovered how difficult it is to make a silk purse out of a sow's ear; the gap between the promise and the reality of continuing inefficiency, jobbery, and the rest of it persisted, as did the problem of attracting talented people from the private sector, where salaries and chances for advancement were so much greater.

Increasingly, Shihab and his associates came to rely upon the *deuxième bureau*, the intelligence service of the army, to wield power, especially after the last day of 1961 when the Syrian Social Nationalist party (PPS), the advocate of a Greater Syria, kidnapped a number of high officers of the army in an attempted coup. The suppression was fierce; more than 6,000 people were arrested, and Camille Chamoun and other opponents of the regime, suspected of involvement, were treated with the greatest suspicion. The army became increasingly visible in the streets of Lebanon, a trend encouraged, to be sure, by the increasing militancy of the Palestinians in Lebanon, and the ordinary civilian was frequently harassed by having to stop at military checkpoints. In spite of this, however, Shihab's supporters believed he was still popular enough and had adequate support in Parliament to seek a second term in 1964. Like Coriolanus (or de Gaulle), however, Shihab resisted this temptation—wisely, some believed, as the alternative might have led to the disintegration of Lebanese democracy.

Charles Hilu attempted to continue the *nahj* and for a brief period gained laurels by purging the administration of incompetence, but, lacking a popular base, he was seen as increasingly the creature of the *deuxième bureau*. In 1970, his candidate as successor, Sarkis, director of the Central Bank, was defeated by Franjiyya, although by the slim margin of one vote. Members of the *deuxième bureau* were prosecuted for corruption; some were purged. In the face of spreading social turbulence and violence, the army was somewhat demoralized. To optimists, freedom now had replaced authoritarianism; to pessimists, the usual social anarchy and insouciance had replaced responsibility and discipline, although Franjiyya did for a period attempt to cultivate an image of social concern by appointing a cabinet of "experts" under Sa'b Salam to monitor the prices of medicines, to impose import duties on luxury goods, and to rationalize the educational system. Little came of these efforts, in part because Lebanon had by then entered a period of increasing turbulence and chaos.

In retrospect, one might say that the Shihab experiment had served to make the Lebanese more aware of the need for social justice and had educated them to an appreciation of the connection between social justice and national stability. After him, many Lebanese were willing to consider the need to limit the excesses of untrammeled laissez-faire, as was evident in some of the measures Franjiyya sought to implement, even if not very effectively. The chief criticism of Shihabism by one of Shihab's leading opponents, Camille Chamoun, was directed not at his social program but at his having led Lebanon "off the tracks" by aligning the country for political reasons so closely to Egypt and to its ambassador to Lebanon, referred to sarcastically at the time as "High-Commissioner of the United Arab Republic of Lebanon." Chamoun also expressed shock that officers who had defied his orders in 1958 were now put into positions of power and honor, a step, he maintained, that undermined any respect for Lebanon's sovereignty. On the other hand, Kamal Joumblatt, a fierce spokesman for radical social reform, paid Shihab tribute during the Civil War:

> No one really thought about the masses. President Shihab had started to awaken an interest in them, but had been unable to complete his work. However, he certainly set the stage for a social policy, and he said at the end of his term: "If the rich continue to hold on to their privileges against everything and against all, there will be a social revolution in Lebanon." We are now living this revolution, one that is both democratic and social; it would have been very useful to have been able to complete it. Syria, however, has given us neither the time nor the means.[8]

Foreign observers have tended to be quite negative regarding the *nahj*. Bent Hansen, for example, said of Lebanon after the experiment that education from the point of view of development remained "entirely inadequate" and that almost everything still needed to be done "to overcome the backwardness of the countryside." He found that hardly any use had yet been made of the waters of the Litani project.[9] And Michael Hudson wrote: "But Chehab was unable to effect lasting changes in the system, which, because of its immobilizing proportionalism and its contributed traditional elitism, proved to be immune to reform by evolutionary means."[10]

Hansen's judgment may be too harsh—the Litani was exploited, for example, to a degree—but it is true that the Litani project hardly had met the expectations at its inception in 1955, when the International Bank lent Lebanon $27 million for the project. The aim then was to double Lebanon's electricity supply. As for the effort by President Hilu to reform the administration, 150 civil servants were "retired" in 1965–1966, but opposition forced the resignation of the Karami extraparliamentary government and the institution of a safer cabinet appointed exclusively from the Parliament (except for Philippe Taqla as foreign minister). Purges by Hilu, dubbed "the Tiger" at the time, came to an end. Another sign of *plus ça change* . . . was the combined success of the National Liberals and the Kata'ib in blocking an effort to increase Muslim representation in the administration (as well as to extend citizenship to a number of Muslims who had long been resident in Lebanon) in February 1974.

SINCE 1975

Lebanon's prosperity continued, in spite of growing social anarchy after 1967, but inflation grew as a threat both to the economy and to social stability and contributed, even if only peripherally, to the final breakdown of 1975.

Since 1975, so great has been the economic as well as political dislocation of the country that data are unreliable and speculative. But one clear, salient feature of the years between 1976 and 1982 was that in the private sector, in spite of chaos, prosperity has continued and in some cases even increased—a tribute to this enterprising people. The losses to most people, however, and the nation as a whole, were devastating.

Losses from the Civil War were in the range of $5 billion. By 1977, according to one study of Lebanon's current economy,[11] the GNP was LL 8.5 billion; although this was not much less than the figure of LL 9 billion for 1974, the Lebanese pound had lost half its value. Inflation between 1975 and 1979 rose some 113 percent (the figure for salaries was only 91 percent). The drop in industrial activity was 40–50 percent. Half of Beirut's 100 hotels (of 1974) had been destroyed; tourism, which had accounted for 20 percent of GNP before the Civil War, had fallen to near zero by 1976. Loss in commercial activity amounted to some LL 3 billion; loss in buildings to some LL 1 billion. Among the 200,000 to 250,000 who had migrated, permanently or temporarily, were 30 percent of Lebanon's construction workers and 32 percent of its industrial workers. One estimate is that Lebanon's population, about 3 million in 1974, had fallen to about 2.6 million in 1979 (2.26 million if nonnationals are excluded). In 1979 some 100,000 Lebanese were employed in Saudi Arabia alone.

Other losses from the Civil War included a drop between 1974 and 1977 of 50 percent in passengers through the International Airport; and during the same period the cargo handled by the port and the number of ships that visited Beirut fell by the same percentage. Twenty-five foreign banks had shifted their area headquarters to Athens, Cairo, or the Gulf. By February 1976, twenty-six banks had been partly or completely destroyed and many vaults had been rifled (curiously, only 7–8 percent of deposits were withdrawn). Fifteen Lebanese banks had moved their operations abroad, mostly to Paris. By 1977 banking operations were 40–50 percent of what they had been before the war. And agricultural production had fallen in all sectors; the production of potatoes, for example, which had been 117,000 metric tons in 1973, fell to 80,000 metric tons in 1974, and tomato production fell from 70,000 metric tons in 1974 to 60,000 in 1975.

Unemployment in 1978 stood at 270,000, and in this year the Israeli invasion, a sequel to the Civil War, cost Lebanon $30 million in the citrus and tobacco crop by preventing harvesting. Industry in 1977 operated at only one-third of its capacity. In Lebanon as a whole 145 hotels had been damaged, at a loss of LL 218 million; in Beirut the number of hotels had declined from 130 (with 10,486 beds) to 44 (4,631 beds) by the end of 1975. Inflation was 85–90 percent a year and continued to be a serious problem through 1982.

In spite of this bleak picture, however, business in the private sector has thrived in all sorts of ways, many of them illegal or at least extralegal—for example, black market operations, smuggling, and the trade in the hashish of the Biqa'. Hashish production began to boom during the Civil War when law enforcement, only halfhearted even in normal times, became impossible. One estimate is that the yearly crop rose from 30,000 metric tons to some 100,000, stimulated by the increase in price from $65 to $150 per kilogram. Operated by about twenty clans and some leading politicians, the production of hashish involves most of the some 100,000 residents of the northern Biqa', where it grows in abundance and from where it is smuggled out through Turkey and Syria and from some small clandestine airports.

Legal operations included entertainment. The new $25 million Summerland seaside resort in west Beirut, which was to be devastated in the summer of 1982, was previously crowded with customers. A LL 100 million luxury marina was planned for a site 20 miles (32 kilometers) north of Beirut; its apartments, costing LL 400,000 to LL 700,000 each, were rapidly bought up in advance. In 1981 more banks were in operation than had been the case before the war, when there had been eighty-six, and bank deposits kept rising (from some $2.76 billion before the Civil War to some $5 billion). Many concerns that had moved their operations abroad—eleven Lebanese banks were in France in 1981–continued to operate, and small industries in processed foods and textiles continued to function and to contribute some 73 percent of the value of Lebanon's exports. The Lebanese pound, well backed by gold, retained its solidity. Gold and foreign exchange reserves stood at LL 2,255.2 million in 1978. Remittances continued to arrive; one estimate of the average remittance from 150,000 expatriates was $1,000 per month, an annual total of almost $2 billion.[12] So also, unfortunately, did large sums of money from foreign governments enter to finance the plethora of combatants. Lebanon was awash with money, and land values soared at least 300–600 percent; one estimate has been up to 1,000 percent! And this investment spread to the countryside, to which some enterprises had moved for safety reasons. Jounieh, port and capital of the Kata'ib-controlled Mountain, was by way of becoming a metropolis, resplendent with boutiques, hotels, and casinos.

And even where disaster struck, business continued through thick and thin—in the case of the Beirut port, so often strafed, bombed, and plundered, because of the determination of those who controlled the port—the Baltaji brothers, Ibrahim and Hassan, the self-declared "*mafiosi*" of the longshoremen, and Henri Pharaon, the port's owner, who used his political savvy and influence on both sides to keep conflict to a minimum. For example, the Kata'ibis,—those who most frequently shelled the port—were included in the sharing of port profits; and whereas the dockworkers were almost all Muslims before the Civil War, the Christians now constituted some 50 percent. Here again, profit made for strange bedfellows, or to put it more optimistically, profit served to provide at least a minimum of integration among the Lebanese.

All was not easy, of course, for profiteers; although taxes could be easily evaded, buying protection was costly, the real estate boom was an unhealthy sign of a lack of confidence in more productive forms of investment, and some wealth came simply from exploiting the virtual collapse of the national public sector. The unreliable supply of water encouraged the import of well-drilling equipment, for example, and the unsteady supply of electricity, the import of small generators for private use.

While the private sector, in however bizarre a way, thrived, the public sector, in spite of the efforts of the Council of Reconstruction and Development (under Muhammad Atallah) and the Bank of Lebanon (under Michel Khuri), as well as organizations such as the Committee for the Reconstruction of Beirut City Center, marked time. The main difficulty, other than the continuing anarchy in the country, was that the government was capital poor. Tax evasion was blatant, and smuggling denied the government many customs receipts. Much of these receipts, constituting some 46 percent of government income in normal times, was now lost to the eighteen illegal ports and piracy. The budget deficit for 1981 was about 35 percent of the total budget. Some aid was coming, however, from other Arab states, and various plans were being devised to integrate private and public efforts to reconstruct the economy when conditions allowed. Foreign companies—there had been 250 U.S. companies in Lebanon in 1975, only 10 in 1978—were beginning to return, however tentatively.

The cost of rebuilding the nation, however, and of resettling the thousands of internal refugees would require tens of billions of dollars, and often destruction outpaced construction. One initiative on the part of the government, in the spirit of Shihab's *nahj* and to meet the unprecedented challenges of the moment, was to provide for a much more active governmental role in the economy. Development plans in 1979 included seventeen different projects to be completed over a five-year period. In 1981–1982 a $4.7 billion nationwide waste management plan was projected, and a large cement factory in Sibline, 24 miles (40 kilometers) south of Beirut, was launched, to employ some 600. The initiative appeared to be there; the question now was whether there would ever be a genuine government again.

Whatever the prospects had been for any genuine economic recovery before June 1982, however, they were set back by the Israeli invasion. Damages the Civil War and its sequels had produced were now multiplied as heavy cannons and Phantoms were added to mortars and Kalashnikovs as agents of destruction. By the end of June at least one-third of Tyre lay in rubble. Rough estimates put the damage there at $75 million, that in Sidon at $100 million. Through July and August much of west Beirut was also being reduced to rubble, and more destruction was to come. One reporter wrote of the "instant archaeology of destruction," a new science to date Lebanon's layers of ruin.[13]

Harbingers of the future were the extension of roads into southern

Lebanon from Israel, the posting of signs in Hebrew, talk of repairing the three miles of track connecting the old coastal railway from Israel north, and the appearance on the Lebanese market of Israeli food produce. By July concern was already being expressed that local Lebanese merchants were being threatened with Israeli competition, and there were even threats to the banking system of Lebanon when, in Sidon, Israeli authorities asked banks to break the secrecy act and disclose the accounts of political organizations. The Central Bank blocked this effort for the moment, but the signs were ominous. In July an office of El-Al was opened in Sidon, and Lebanese began to visit Israel as tourists.

But in spite of the cataclysmic events of June and July, the Lebanese entrepreneurial spirit thrived. A Lebanese businessman said that rather than being concerned primarily about the fifth Arab-Israeli war, his colleagues were only "thinking about land."[14] One investor was reported to have sold a property he had bought in 1977 for LL 350,000 at LL 4 million! At the same time, Mitri Noamar, Beirut's mayor, was talking of plans to build, over the ruins of old Beirut, a new Paris![15]

NOTES

1. *L'Orient–Le Jour*, March 17, 1974.
2. Joseph Malone, "Lebanon," in *The Arab Lands of Western Asia* (Englewood Cliffs, N.J.: Prentice-Hall, 1973), pp. 1–35.
3. Nadim Khalaf, *Economic Implications of the Size of Nations with Special Reference to Lebanon* (Leiden: Brill, 1971).
4. Yusif Sayigh, *Entrepreneurs of Lebanon: The Role of the Business Leader in a Developing Economy* (Cambridge, Mass.: Harvard University Press, 1962).
5. Michael Hudson, "The Lebanese Crisis: The Limits of Consociational Democracy," *Journal of Palestine Studies*, Spring-Summer 1976, pp. 109–122.
6. Samih K. Farsoun, "Family Structure and Society in Modern Lebanon," in Louise E. Sweet, ed., *Peoples and Cultures of the Middle East: Volume II: Life in Cities, Towns and Countryside* (New York: Natural History Press, 1970), pp. 257–307.
7. See Iliya Harik, *Lebanon: Anatomy of a Conflict*, American Universities Field Staff Reports, Asia Series, No. 49, 1981.
8. Kamal Joumblatt, *Pour le Liban* [In behalf of Lebanon] (Paris: Stock, 1978), p. 114.
9. Bent Hansen, "Middle East Development Prospects—What It Looked Like in 1973," in Abraham Becker et al., *The Economics and Politics of the Middle East* (New York: American Elsevier, 1975), pp. 3–37.
10. Michael Hudson, *Arab Politics: The Search for Legitimacy* (New Haven, Conn.: Yale University Press, 1977), p. 291.
11. Sélim Turquié, "De quoi vivent les libanais?" [How do the Lebanese live?], *Monde Diplomatique*, October 1979, pp. 1 and 6.
12. David Ignatius, *Wall Street Journal*, December 22, 1980.
13. William Farrell, *New York Times*, July 13, 1982.
14. David Ignatius, *Wall Street Journal*, July 13, 1982.
15. *Christian Science Monitor*, July 13, 1982.

5

Polity and Politics

Politically, the Republic of Lebanon has been a product of its long experience of multiethnic coexistence (when this worked), of particular institutions and traditions elaborated under the mandate system, and of an agreement, the National Pact, couched inevitably in negative rather than positive terms. On the positive side, this legacy provided for freedom and for participation in the affairs of state by all groups, although in a descending scale of effective power. On the negative side, the peculiar system of checks and balances explicit or implicit in the system has often made for immobilism, log-rolling, compromise where decisiveness is called for, the resort to *wasta* (special personal influence), and the inability of leaders to make forceful decisions without putting the whole structure at risk. As a result, the freedom the system has offered has depended on luck and good fortune to a large extent, on economic prosperity, a favorable and calm international atmosphere, and the predisposition of stronger neighbors and the great powers to tolerate or to protect Lebanon.

Internally, the government of Lebanon has been kept weak by the primacy of primordial loyalties over loyalty to the state, of transnational loyalties and connections, of the easy resort to the use of the pressure of the "street" (or of the university campus), and of the resort of some, and then virtually all, groups to the recruitment and employment of extralegal militias. The system has sometimes been described as a government of men rather than of laws; often one heard, even before 1975, the lament "ma fi dawla . . . ma fi hukume"—there is no state, there is no government. The most powerful figure in the republic, the president, has usually ended his career in disappointment and rejection. Khuri was forced out of power by a national strike; Chamoun left office in the wake of a civil war; Shihab, in some ways the most effective of them all, had to resort to increasingly unpopular police methods to enforce his progressive program, a program that rapidly lost most of its effectiveness under his ideological successor, Charles Hilu. And the

77

Franjiyya regime ended in the chaos of the Civil War. After 1976 the incumbent, Sarkis, presided over a phantom government.

But in spite of all these flaws in the system, some important changes did occur over the decades between 1943 and 1975. In 1952 women were given the vote and a secret ballot was provided for. As already discussed, the Shihab regime was by no means barren of creative legislation, and even under Franjiyya some important issues—education, in particular—were seriously addressed, if hardly solved. There was some room, even if this was constrained, for political creativity within the framework of the constitution. Surveys made by the Smocks and by Iliya Harik in the early 1970s indicated that the higher the level of education, the greater the Lebanese identification among Muslims as well as Christians; and among both religious groups there was basic agreement over preserving Lebanon's free-enterprise system.[1]

INSTITUTIONS

According to the Constitution of 1926, the president is the kingpin of the system. Under him are the army and its intelligence service, national security (the Sûreté Générale), and the special riot police force (Squad 16). He has the power to apply "urgent" legislation by decree (Article 58), veto bills (Article 27), dissolve parliament, and appoint and dismiss his prime minister (traditionally a Sunnite) and the cabinet (traditionally appointed to reflect sectarian distribution). And he also has had considerable informal power through patronage that deputies depended upon and the possibility of influencing elections through pressures by the *deuxième bureau* and the army. It has been estimated that under normal circumstances he could sway about one-third of the parliamentary elections.

The president is elected by parliament, serves a single six-year term (unless the Constitution is amended to allow for another term, as was the case with Bishara Khuri), and must, by tradition, be a Maronite. To be elected, a presidential candidate needs a two-thirds parliamentary vote on the first vote, a simple majority on the subsequent vote. Before the 1982 election, the question arose whether the required two-thirds should be of the original ninety-nine deputies or of the remaining ninety-two—parliamentary elections had not been feasible since 1975.

The president's powers, extraordinary on paper, have nevertheless been circumscribed by realities. Unless he wanted to risk losing the support of the bulk of the Muslim community, he would appoint a Sunnite prime minister who had influence and prestige in his community. Thus, Franjiyya, as the nation was skidding to disaster, was virtually forced to appoint Rashid Karami premier even though there was bad blood between them. Chamoun earlier had lost favor with many Muslims by keeping as his prime minister a political neutral, Sami Sulh, whom he consigned largely to the wings. And the president has had to appoint a well-balanced cabinet to obtain parliamentary approval and to satisfy the important segments of the population. One example would be the cabinet appointed by Sarkis in 1979, which included three Sunnites, two Shi'ites, two Maronites, two Greek Orthodox, one Greek Catholic, and one Druze.

The president has also had to reckon with the various business and professional organizations and, even within his own community, he has had to take the patriarchate of the Maronite Church into account. The church is very wealthy, incidentally, owning 20 percent of the land, and through its priests it can wield considerable influence in local Maronite communities. In 1958, as already seen, the patriarch played an important role in Chamoun's eventual defeat. And, as was seen in both 1952 and 1958, to the chagrin of Khuri and then Chamoun, the president has had to keep the loyalty of his commander in chief. And he has had to reckon with the mainly Maronite Kata'ib party, probably the best-organized party in the land, with the best-trained militia. It was this party that in September 1958 forced the new president, Shihab, to revise his cabinet in a more balanced fashion.

The prime minister, as indicated, has been expected by his Sunnite community to be a man who commanded influence and respect. Otherwise the Sunnites would feel that they were not adequately represented in the power structure. In addition, for the same reason, the prime minister had to be perceived to play an important role in the government and be shown due respect, as was demonstrated in the events following the crisis of April 1973. After Israeli commandos had managed to assassinate three prominent Palestinian leaders in the heart of Beirut, the Salam government resigned because the prime minister claimed the army had refused to obey orders to resist the Israelis. Thereupon Franjiyya appointed a political nonentity, Amin al-Hafiz, as prime minister. Both the Shi'ite imam and the Sunnite grand mufti, among other Muslim leaders, protested this appointment. At the same time serious clashes between the army and the Palestinians broke out, Syria closed its borders with Lebanon, and Sa'iqa, the Syrian-controlled Palestinian militia, went into action along the border. Through Arab mediation, however, the state of emergency that had been called was ended. Hafiz withdrew his candidacy for the premiership—he had never been confirmed by Parliament—and a much stronger Muslim leader, Takieddin Sulh, was finally able to form an acceptable cabinet, but only with difficulty and much haggling. Subsequently Syria opened its border again. The power of prime ministers has varied, but overall their influence has increased.

By 1974, for example, it had become customary for all legislation to be countersigned by the prime minister, providing him with a veto.

It has been very difficult to form cabinets that are adequately representative of real power and that can win the approval of parliament and satisfy each sectarian group. They have been subject to so many pressures and shifting alignments on the political scene that they have seldom enjoyed longevity. Malcolm Kerr has observed that between 1926 and 1964 the average life of each cabinet was less than eight months.[2] On the other hand, many of the same men returned to their posts (only so many people with the necessary clout being available) in the new cabinets; between 1926 and 1963, 333 ministerial posts were occupied by 134 individuals.

Cabinets have tended to be weak; they have been dependent upon the cooperation of the president, and frequently the cabinet minister has been more interested in serving his constituency and his own image than he is in serving the state. Intracabinet rivalries have been a common occurrence. From 1960 to 1964, for example, while Pierre Gemayel and Kamal Joumblatt were in the same cabinet, much of their energy was expended in attacks upon one another, the first in his party paper *Al-Amal*, the second through his paper *Al-Anba*. And in 1975, Prime Minister Rashid Karami complained that his own minister of the interior, Camille Chamoun, was engaging in civil war! Cabinets, in short, have not been effective; they have tended to reflect the tensions and rivalries of the parliament and of the nation at large. On occasion, a president would appoint a cabinet consisting wholly or partly of extraparliamentary persons, of "technocrats," for example, as Ilyas Sarkis did in 1976. The purpose of this was to depoliticize the administration of the nation and to provide for expertise. Such cabinets, however, have been vulnerable to harassment from deputies in parliament who naturally have felt that their influence and patronage have been clipped.

Parliament, or more accurately the Chamber of Deputies, renamed in 1979 the National Assembly, is elected every four years by popular vote to represent the nation in accordance with the size and distribution of the various sects. Each slot has been assigned to one sect or another, according to its presence and size in any given constituency, and has been part of the "list" of any one bloc. An imaginary constituency might consist of 1,000 Maronites, 500 Greek Orthodox, 250 Greek Catholics, and 250 Sunnites. In this case rival lists would consist of 4 Maronites, 2 Greek Orthodox, 1 Greek Catholic, and 1 Sunnite. In each case the competition for office would be intrasectarian and not between people of different sects, a factor for integration. It has been possible to vote across lists, but this has usually not been done. In 1968, for example, fourteen of twenty-five lists were elected *in toto* (one district was represented by a single member).

Each list has been strenuously negotiated by leaders of each community to ensure that their list obtains the majority of votes; this in turn has meant that the leader of each confessional group would make sure that his running mates from the other confessions had sufficient popularity to help the whole list win. This system has made for compromise and integration as well as for moderation and, often, for noncontroversial mediocrity. To avoid a proliferation of candidates, a person choosing to run has had to deposit $1,000, which he would forfeit should he win less than 25 percent of the vote. Elections have been dramatic and often chaotic events; pressures of all sorts have been brought to bear, and victories have often been celebrated by firing guns into the air and burning tires in the streets. An important role has been played by toughs known as *qabada'i*s, whose job has been to keep supporters of the boss's list in line and properly bused to their native villages, where they vote; it has also been an occasion to discourage opponents from voting by strong-arm methods, if necessary. Not strangely, the army has been called upon, on the four successive Sundays when elections were held in one part or another of Lebanon, to supervise the elections and to reduce violence to a minimum.

Originally (between 1943 and 1947) there were only five electoral districts, which gave the powerful *za'im* of his area considerable power to manipulate the Grand List, as it was called. A step toward democratization was to enlarge the number of districts as well as the number of deputies, but these have also been decreased on occasion to suit the interests of the incumbents at the time. In 1951 the number of districts was increased to nine, the number of deputies from fifty-five to seventy-seven. In 1953, the number of deputies was reduced to forty-four, the number of districts expanded to thirty-three. In 1957, the number of deputies was reduced to sixty-six, of districts to twenty-five; and in 1960, the present system, the number of deputies was increased to ninety-nine (the number of districts increased by one). It will be noted that the number of seats has always been a multiple of eleven, reflecting the formula of five Muslims to six Christians.

Unless the president has chosen to dissolve parliament unexpectedly, the deputy elected holds office for a four-year period. Perhaps his most important function has been to participate in the election of the next president. Every six years, when these elections have taken place, summers have often been "hot," and it has not been unknown for deputies to come to the vote armed. Normally voting has been public, but the election of the president (or the vote on his dismissal

TABLE 5.1   Distribution of Seats in
Parliament in 1960

Maronites	30
Sunnites	20
Shi'ites	19
Greek Orthodox	11
Druzes	6
Greek Catholics	6
Armenian Orthodox	4
Minorities	3

if he is accused of treason or the violation of the constitution) has been secret.

Using the election of 1968 as base, Iliya Harik has determined that membership of the elite "establishment" that parliament has tended to be included ten members of the old aristocratic families whose power was broken in the nineteenth century and about twenty "notables" (men with a particular traditional or religious importance in their districts); the rest of the ninety-nine deputies represented economic power, education, and professional training. Allowing for overlapping in occupations, in the parliament of 1968 there were ten landlords, forty-four lawyers, seventeen businessmen, and twenty-eight professionals. The average deputy was educated (70 percent had university degrees), economically active, and of middle or upper income. Deputies did not constitute any sort of oligarchy; turnover in each election is about 45 percent (compared with 15 percent in the United States and 28 percent in Great Britain). Frequently election to parliament has been a steppingstone to the cabinet, and it has conferred considerable influence on the incumbent because of favors he could bestow upon members of his constituency.

An important point to notice about the "establishment" is that, because the deputies have been elected according to a system that has *not* pitted sect against sect, and because the lead man on any list has been chosen as the man most likely to capture votes for the list independent of sectarian considerations, members of parliament have tended to cooperate within the confines of their own parties and blocs regardless of sect. Malcolm Kerr has suggested that this system, in effect, has meant that the *millet* system of Ottoman days, when political rivalries took place within and not between confessional groups, continued in the modern Lebanese system.[3] But in two areas it has been possible for sectarian groups to confront each other directly—administration and foreign policy. For example, a frequent source of crisis has been the demand of one sect or another for greater participation in civil service appointments; in the case of foreign policy, it has already been seen—as in the strife of 1957–1958 when to some Muslims, Chamoun seemed to be violating the National Pact by placing Maronite interests above national interests—a direct confrontation between Muslim and Christian sects can occur. Another source of crisis has been the issue of the census and the knowledge that a new census would show that a redistribution of positions of power is in order, a proposition most Christians would find intolerable.

As Harik has observed, Parliament in alliance with the president has been able, in critical but not chaotic times, to contain powerful forces such as the *deuxième bureau*, which was purged in 1970–1971.[4] Weaknesses of this institution are that it has excluded the lower orders, peasants, and workers; that deputies, beholden to their districts, have tended to think and to act with local rather than national interests in mind (in 1968 only one-third of the candidates stood as members of parties); and that it has for the most part excluded representation by ideologically oriented and radical parties.

Appointments to administrative positions, until 1959, were made within each ministry; informally, but not by law, confessional distribution had always to be taken into account. In 1959, the new Personnel Law did provide formally for an equitable distribution of appointments, and in principle, Muslims and Christians have since then been appointed on the basis of parity, rather than according to the 6 : 5 formula. In the same year the Public Service Council was established to supervise the examining, the training, and the certifying of new appointees, and the National Institute of Administration was established to provide for administrative training. Most students of the Lebanese scene, however, would agree that because of political pressures, *wasta*, and patronage, the Lebanese administrative system has lacked integrity and efficiency. In addition, distribution of appointments has continued to be inequitable. Although proportionally more Shi'ites, for example, have been recruited since independence, the distribution of appointments has been only moderately readjusted. In 1955, 40 percent of the civil servants in higher administrative positions were Maronites (with 30 percent of the population) and 27 percent to Sunnites (with 20 percent of the population). The Shi'ites, with 18 percent of the population, held only 3.6 percent of such positions. On the eve of the Civil War, the proportions were essentially the same.

Government in Lebanon, reflecting its Ottoman and French legacies, has been highly centralized. The five provincial governors (*muhafazes*), and the district prefects (the *qaimaqams*) who have administered the *muhafazat*s and the *qada*s, respectively, have come under the Ministry of the Interior. This ministry, and the other ministries in their particular spheres, have held the purse strings. Only minor local matters have been dealt with by elected village and town councils.

Justice has been supervised by the Ministry of Justice, but the real authority has been the Supreme Council of Justice, which has consisted of eleven judges appointed by the government. It has jurisdiction over the various judges, whom it has appointed and whom it could transfer. Beneath it have been fifty-six Single Judge Courts (seventeen in Beirut) of first instance; eleven Courts of Appeal (five in Beirut), with three judges on each; and four Courts of Cassation (three dealing with commercial cases, one with criminal cases). Other courts have included the Judiciary Council (which deals with cases of public security and includes the president of the Court of Cassation and four other judges appointed by the government); the State Council (with six judges), which can annul administrative decrees; and the Administrative Division, which deals with administrative principles. Other courts have dealt with specialized areas, the military, the press, and commerce, for example. The system of justice has been based upon codes adapted from European nations (property, obligation and contracts, civil procedure, maritime, penal, military penal, and criminal instruction). Penal procedure is an adaptation of the Ottoman law.

In matters of personal status, however, which involves questions of inheritance and marriage, justice has been dealt with by the different religious organizations. The Shi'ites have had courts of first instance and one of appeal, which have functioned according to the Ja'fari school of law (*Sharia'*). The Sunnites have had their own courts of first instance and one of appeal. Status law has varied considerably: Among the Shi'ites, for example, claims to an inheritance are based on the closeness of relationship to the dead person; among Sunnites a daughter inherits only half as much as a son, and a person can will only one-third of his wealth at his discretion unless he has the approval of the legal heirs. The Druzes have had personal status courts, appeal has been to the top Shaikh al-'Aql whom particular Druzes have recognized as their leader (at one time there were three such claimants).

Christians also have had their own courts and provisions for appeal. It is interesting that the highest courts of appeal have sometimes lain outside Lebanon. The Maronites, for example, could appeal to Rome; the Greek Orthodox to the Patriarchal Court in Damascus; and the Greek Catholics to the Patriarchal Court in Cairo or, finally, to Rome.

In their intercourse with the government the religious groups have been represented by their hierarchies: For example, the Sunnites have been represented by the Supreme Islamic Council under its grand mufti;

the Shi'ites, since 1969, by the Higher Shi'ite Council, which has elected its own president.

PARTIES

Except for the Kata'ib, its Muslim counterpart the Najjadah (Helpers), the Armenian Tashnaq, and one or two minor groups, most political parties in Lebanon have been loose coalitions gathered around powerful figures—the za'ims. Some of the leaders have not even belonged to particular parties; allegiance to the leaders has been based purely on their particular influence. Thus, in the parliament of 1960, Rashid Karami could count upon four to six deputies to support him, Kamal al-As'ad on six to eight, and so forth. Some twenty deputies could be considered as "independents." The only important cohesive "modern" party, the Kata'ib, was represented by only nine members in parliament in 1968, seven in 1972. Coalition making between these various components has usually depended upon particular issues; to an outsider the impression is kaleidoscopic.

The za'im has had to be a rich man to keep his clientele in line with favors, and he has had to be influential—as prime minister, Rashid Karami was able to serve his community well and gain support by establishing the regular trade fair in Tripoli. And za'imship has often been inherited—thus Emile Bustani's daughter Myrna was able to succeed him in Parliament, Walid Joumblatt succeeded his father as leader of the Progressive Socialist party as well as communal Druze leader, and Bashir Gemayel replaced his father Pierre as the leading figure in the Kata'ib.

Almost all the parties and establishment figures represented in Parliament have accepted the status quo and the rules of the game, whatever some might say publicly for electoral purposes. One maverick was Kamal Joumblatt, enfant terrible of the establishment and spokesman for the transformation of the system into a secular state, radical reform in the administration, and for full alignment of Lebanon with the Palestinian and Arab causes. (Joumblatt will be considered more fully below.)

Ideologically, in direct contrast and frequent confrontation with Joumblatt was Pierre Gemayel, the founder and leader of the mainly Maronite Phalangist party, the Kata'ib. This party was established in 1936, partly on the model of some European fascist groups of the period, in reaction to the Pan-Syrian PPS of Antun Saadah, which was considered a danger to Lebanese sovereignty, and to the demands of some Muslim leaders that parts of Greater Lebanon be reincorporated into Syria. The Kata'ib's goal was to organize and train resistance to any threat to the

TABLE 5.2   Estimated Party Power in the Parliament Elected in 1960

Party	Number of Deputies Who Might Be Counted On
Constitutional Union party (Bishara Khuri)	4-8
National Bloc party (Raymond Iddi)	5-6
National Liberal party (Camille Chamoun)	4-5
Kata'ib (Pierre Gemayel)	7-8
Progressive Socialist party (Kamal Joumblatt)	5-8
Al-Najjadah (Adnan Hakim)	1-2
Tashnaq (Armenian)	4

Source: Michael Hudson, The Precarious Republic: Modernization in Lebanon (New York: Random House, 1968).

integrity and special personality of Lebanon. In the 1970s it may have had a membership of 65,000, and it boasted a well-disciplined militia of some 10,000 (in 1977 it claimed to be able to bring some 40,000 combatants into the field). The party has been highly centralized, with authority descending pyramidally down from the governing politburo. The party has been a fierce defender of the status quo and a firm opponent of the armed Palestinian presence in Lebanon. It made use of its military clout in the latter stages of the 1958 civil strife; in 1969 and after, in confrontation with Palestinian units; and in 1975, when it took the lead in the Civil War against both the Lebanese left and the Palestinians. By 1982 it was in virtually full command of most of the Mountain, the center of opposton to both the Palestinians and, since 1976, to the Syrian presence in Lebanon.

Pierre Gemayel has not been the only spokesman or leading figure of the Maronite community. Camille Chamoun and his National Liberal party (the Ahrar), which has stood ideologically for many of the same ideals as the Kata'ib, have also been important. Different in orientation has been Raymond Iddi, son of Emile Iddi, who was president during the mandatory period. From his point of view and that of his associate, his brother Pierre, a prominent banker, the Kata'ib has appeared to be a faintly fascist organization, drawing upon the narrow prejudices of the lower middle class. His own party, the National Bloc, stood for a much greater openness to the Arab world and a greater willingness to come to terms with the Palestinians.

Very much a son of Lebanon, Raymond Iddi, patrician of Jbeil, has attempted to become president like his father; but because of his relatively small following and his association with France (rather than the more powerful United States), he has never proved successful. In 1976 he was defeated by Franjiyya. Like many other politicians of his class, he was educated in law at Saint Joseph, and although he of course speaks colloquial Arabic, his language of culture is French (as was true of Fuad Shihab, Charles Hilu, and others). As a deputy, and sometimes as a member of different cabinets, he played a major role in promoting Lebanon as a banking center by providing for a law guaranteeing secrecy to depositors, and he helped create the elite police force, Squad 16. He has always taken independent stands, denouncing the Cairo Agreement of 1969 (which provided for a modus vivendi between the PLO and the Lebanese government), for example, because he argued that this would provide a basis for the Israeli occupation of the south. His solution was to have the U.N. patrol the border.

Although he supported Franjiyya's candidacy in 1970, he soon became a bitter critic of the new regime. In 1975 he attacked the United States for allegedly plotting to have Lebanon partitioned, the Palestinians crushed, and Lebanon made a series of satellites of Israel. Since 1975, he has strongly opposed Christian extremists who favor partition, and he has stood for reconciliation with the Palestinians and with the Arab world in general. In March 1976, when at least six separate armies were operating in Lebanon, he declared: "It's becoming a vaudeville act. Nothing is serious in my country." And after a number of attempts on his life, and having been branded by his enemies as "Muhammad" Iddi, the Amid (dean), as he was also once called, went into exile in Paris, from where he has roundly denounced the Syrian intrusion and predicted that Lebanon might now never regain its sovereignty—a fear shared by many of his compatriots.

Iddi, Gemayel, and Chamoun have stood firmly for the integrity and independence of Lebanon; some other Christians have regarded Lebanon as an artificial construct, its sovereign existence a barrier to a larger and more just society. Such has been the thesis of the mainly Greek Orthodox Syrian Social Nationalist party, which has played an important role in the life of Lebanon, usually extralegally. This party was founded by the Greek Orthodox ideologue, Antun Saadah, in 1932. As already discussed, its original goal was to integrate Lebanon into a Greater Syria and to revitalize this nation through discipline according to the "leader principle," by which all decisions are made by the leader at the top. Twice this party attempted to take power by coup d'état, in 1949 when Prime Minister Riad Sulh had Saadah executed (only to pay for this with his own life in 1951, when he was assassinated in retaliation) and in 1961 when the party was ruthlessly suppressed by the Lebanese army. From 1962 to 1969 the party was illegal. It has never regained its previous influence, but it has survived and has continued to play a role in the Lebanese polity. By 1977 it had split into three groups, a Maoist wing in Jordan (under Asad al-Ashkar), an extreme right wing (under Georges 'Abd al-Masih), and the majority (under Inam Ra'd), which has been opened to the idea of Arabism and which, in the Civil War, supported the opposition National Front.

Also transnational in orientation have been small parties allied to non-Lebanese governments, usually in favor of some version of Pan-Arabism. These parties have usually been grouped with the left, although some of them, especially the "Nasserist" groups, have in fact been ideologically "bourgeois." A considerable number of parties have made use of Nasser's name—among them the Independent Nasserist Movement, the Popular Nasserist Organization, and the Nasserist Organization—Corrective Movement—he remains a much more popular legend among Lebanese Muslims than elsewhere.

An important and growing movement has been the Shi'ite Movement of the Deprived (founded in 1974), which had leftist tendencies and which, during the Civil War, was allied with the Syrians. Its militia, al-Amal (hope), has become well-organized and -armed and has played a formidable role on the Lebanese scene.

Arab socialist in orientation have been the local branches of the Ba'th parties, one aligned with Iraq, the other with Iraq's rival, Syria. Marxist in orientation have been the Organization of Communist Action under Muhsin Ibrahim; the pro-Soviet Lebanese Communist party, founded in 1930 and usually banned; and Kamal Joumblatt's Progressive Socialist party. On the eve of the Civil War of 1975, these various parties of the left were combined under the umbrella Front for Progressive Parties and National Forces (FPPNF) under the leadership of Joumblatt.

The Progressive Socialist party, some would argue, was not really Marxist at all. Much of its membership—it claimed some 6,800 members in 1959—was made up of Druzes whose loyalty to Joumblatt was sectarian, not ideological. However, thirteen members of the Council of Leadership were Christians; only two were Druzes (and one Sunnite) in 1959. Although Joumblatt supported Arabist and Palestinian causes, he appeared to be fundamentally a reformist and a Lebanese nationalist. In 1956 he had helped avoid an all-out condemnation of the tripartite invasion of Egypt, for example. And while he advocated the abolition of sectarianism, "feudalism," and public ownership of the major means of production (but not of small personal property), and the adoption of cooperatives, a planned economy, and insurance (health, housing, employment, and so on), he was willing to work within the system and often served as a cabinet minister. Nevertheless, Joumblatt did advocate fundamental and radical reform, and in revolutionary moments, 1958 and 1975, he threw his support to those ready to resort to violence.

The clearly Marxist and revolutionary parties, other than the small Communist party, were descendants of the Arab Nationalist Movement, founded in 1954 at the American University of Beirut by George Habash and a small group of colleagues. Originally the Nationalist Movememnt was essentially Nasserist and Pan-Arabist rather than socialist. After 1967, however, before it split into a number of components, it did become socialist as well as nationalist when Habash became convinced that Palestine could be liberated only through revolution in Beirut as well as in Riyadh and elsewhere in the Arab world. The Arab Nationalist Movement, as such, is now defunct, although the term is still current. Its heirs have been the Arab Socialist Action party, whose military arm is the Popular Front for the Liberation of Palestine (PFLP), both under Habash; the Organisation of Lebanese Socialists (OLS), established in 1969, under Muhsin Ibrahim and Muhammad Kishly; and the Popular Democratic Front for the Liberation of Palestine (PDFLP) under Nayif Hawatmeh. It will be noticed that through Habash, in particular, the Palestinian left has been as much an active force in Lebanese politics as it is in the overall Palestinian struggle itself.

The Ba'th party was first officially established in Lebanon in 1949 when a branch was opened, to become, in 1954, a part of the National Command, the top politburo of this Pan-Arabist party. The Ba'th, advocate of the union of all Arab states according to the principles of Arab socialism, does not recognize the authority of separate Arab states as such. When Iraqi and Syrian Ba'th leaders, after taking power in both Syria and Iraq, broke with each other in the early 1960s, two branches of the party appeared in Lebanon, one loyal to Baghdad, the other to Damascus.

Although the left constituted a threat on the eve of the Civil War, and although opinion in some quarters, judging by the election of two of its members to parliament, constituted a growing challenge to the establishment and to the reigning za'ims, one should not exaggerate its power. One estimate has it that it could count upon only 20,000 for solid core support and only some 300,000 to demonstrate for its causes. The left still had arrayed against it the influence of the traditional leaders. In addition, the Lebanese proletariat was small and trade unions were under modern middle-class control. Influential Muslims continue to have a vested interest in the system—in any radical or transnational state they would be small potatoes indeed—and ethnic loyalties and identifications continued to operate.

INTERNATIONAL VULNERABILITY

If the left alone was not a serious threat to the system, however, on the eve of the Civil War it had an imposing ally that it could rely upon, the Palestinians; and because of the porousness of the Lebanese polity, it could count for subvention and for arms upon the more radical Arab states. It could also count on the fact that the Lebanese army, which reflected the Lebanese dichotomy, with most officers being Christian and a slight majority of the regular troops being Muslims, would hesitate to act forcefully in any serious confrontation (as had been the case in 1958). The army, as it turned out, disintegrated in 1976 when some of it aligned with the left and some with the right. Also indicative of Lebanon's vulnerability was the fact that ever since independence, an important factor in its elections has been Cairo and Damascus, and the Lebanese military command was forced in 1969 to come to terms with the Palestinians in Cairo. Syria, in turn, has never (except indirectly) recognized Lebanon's sovereignty and has not even had an embassy in Beirut, and many Lebanese were convinced that Syria (as well as Israel) had irredentist designs upon some or all of Lebanon. By 1976, and until 1982, of course, what law and order Lebanon still enjoyed was provided mainly by the Syrian army.

During the Civil War, Syria initially supported the left and the Palestinians. When Syria reversed its position to shore up the Lebanese Front (comprising groups devoted to the reestablishment of Lebanese integrity and sovereignty—see Table 6.1), Egypt, now Syria's opponent, in the spring of 1976 sent in a thousand-man Palestinian force under Egyptian control to support the left. Another case of Lebanon's vulnerability to the outside was the overflow across its borders of the Iranian revolution of 1978–1979. Not only were the Shi'ites given new heart, but there were several indications of direct interference by Tehran in Lebanon's affairs. In November 1979, for example, fifty Iranian youths from the Arab University of Beirut invaded the grounds of the U.S. Embassy in Beirut until dispersed by Syrian troops; at the same time a number of Iranian volunteers entered Lebanon through Syria to fight for the Palestinians, as was true in June 1982.

Of course, since Lebanon's founding in the seventeenth century, major foreign powers, as well as other Middle Eastern states, have interfered in its internal affairs. A case of this was the role of the United States in 1957–1958. William Crane Eveland has shown in his *Ropes of Sand* (1980) that the U.S. ambassador and the Central Intelligence Agency (CIA) played an important part in the elections of 1957 in order to counter the growing influence of Syria and Egypt. Not only was American money filtered in to influence votes, but the U.S. ambassador pushed President Chamoun into having Charles Malik, virtually a symbol of pro-Westernism, run for parliament against his better judgment that Malik's victory could only be interpreted as overkill. The United States even financed the paying-off of Malik's opponent. Later, Chamoun agreed to consider running for a second term only if he had the full support of the U.S. government, but this he did not receive. After the landing of the U.S. Marines, the new U.S. ambassador decided that U.S. influence should be thrown behind Fuad Shihab and made quite clear to Chamoun that the Americans had landed, not to save him, but to establish a base for possible use should the July revolution in Iraq spread. So blatant, in Eveland's eyes, was such U.S. interference that in 1975 he wrote: "The destruction of Lebanon, which now seems inevitable, was at least in part a result of our meddling" (p. 15). In 1975, important as myth, if not reality, was the conviction of opposition leaders, Kamal Joumblatt among them, that the CIA had poured $200 million into Lebanon to destabilize the nation and bring the PLO to heel.

One student of the Middle East has argued that over its history, Lebanon has been saved from extinction by one external force interfering at the right time to counter another that is threatening Lebanon's integrity. Today, when Lebanon has become an international battlefield, this thesis offers small comfort.

THE PALESTINIAN FACTOR

Serious as external manipulations of the Lebanese scene have been, however, and important as support for the left from radical states has been, the greatest danger to the Lebanese entity has proven to be the Palestinian presence on its soil—that is, until 1976, when it became the Syrian presence, and 1982, the Israeli presence. After 1965, the Palestinians were to become a crucial political factor in Lebanon's life. Up to this time, the refugee community of some 200,000 to 300,000, never recognized as more than transient, consisted of two relatively quiescent groups: the more educated and venturesome (perhaps some 20 percent), who had entered into the Lebanese economic and academic world, generally prospered, and contributed much to the economy and the culture; and those who remained in the tawdry bidonville camps, eking out their existence and grudgingly accepting assistance from the United Nations Relief and Works Agency for Palestine Refugees (UNRWA). Inspired by the mystique of "the Return" to Palestine they opposed any gesture from those who aided them that might indicate any permanence of settlement and even established the Organization for Shattering Refugee Settlement Programs. As nonnationals they needed work permits from the Ministry of Social Affairs to seek employment, and although, if they were employed, they paid into social security, they were not entitled to any of the benefits. The camp dwellers had little reason to be unduly grateful to their Lebanese hosts, except that they had enabled them to survive.

It is important to note that two of the camps, Shatila and Bourj al-Barajna, lay along the strategic main road to the International Beirut Airport and that several in Tyre and Sidon lay in Muslim areas where, as they shared grievances with the local population, a symbiosis took place, dangerous to the state. In the case of some, Tall al-Za'tar in particular, refugees, mainly Shi'ite, from Israeli incursions into the south sought shelter and, when violence started, would often cooperate militarily with the Palestinians. Tall al-Za'tar, in fact, was where the Civil War began, in a certain sense. It was toward this camp that the fateful bus was proceeding on April 13, 1975, when the massacre that precipitated the war took place, and it was the siege of this camp, located in a predominantly Christian area, by the militias of Chamoun and the Kata'ib that led the Palestinians to enter the battle in full force. This siege, one of the bloodier affairs in the Civil War, has given Tall al-Za'tar great symbolic importance to either side. For the one the defense of this well-fortified camp, benefiting from lying astride a complex of British World War II bunkers, was declared to be the Stalingrad of the Palestinians; and the fall of this camp in August 1976 was likened by the other side to the fall of the Bastille. There were about 4,000 casualties in this battle and some outright massacres, and some 12,000 Palestinians fled to other parts of Lebanon. What remained of the camp was razed.

In 1965, when Palestinian commando raids into Israel began from across the Lebanese border as a matter of policy, Lebanese security forces often intercepted them—Arafat himself spent a brief period in a Lebanese jail. In 1966 Jalal Khawash, a commando, died in prison, allegedly at the hands of Lebanese security forces. The incident raised a storm of protest from Palestinians and Lebanese progressives. In March 1968 the brave resistance of Palestinian units (in cooperation with the Jordanian army) at Karamah, Jordan, to an Israeli armed ground attack inspired a fresh wave of recruitment to the Palestinian Resistance Movement and aroused a fresh burst of enthusiasm for the Palestinian cause among Lebanese radicals. But, to the indignation of many Lebanese, even of Kamal Joumblatt and the usually sympathetic citizens of Sidon, some Palestinian groups began to make themselves increasingly visible by defiantly walking armed in public streets, setting up checkpoints, and extracting contributions from passersby. On an analogy with what was happening in Amman, some Lebanese began to see themselves as becoming "Jordanized." Public funerals for Palestinian martyrs and other demonstrations inevitably led to clashes with the army and the Kata'ib after 1969.

One reason for the undisciplined actions of many Palestinian groups was the fact that the Palestinian movement was so fragmented; the PLO was, in effect, an umbrella organization, although its leading element, Yasir Arafat's al-Fatah, was the largest group, with the most money and the greatest clout. Some groups were beholden to particular Arab states, often at odds with one another, and George Habash's militant PFLP was dedicated to the support of the Lebanese left. Efforts to arrange for detente included the signing of the Cairo Agreement in 1969, the basis for all later truces and detentes. This agreement was one of Nasser's last acts as an Arab leader.

The agreement came out of a conference, presided over by the Egyptian leader and including General Emile Bustani, representing Lebanon, and Arafat. Its contents have remained officially secret, but versions of it have been published on occasion. In effect it provided that the Palestinians would be recognized as responsible for order in their camps and be allowed "to participate in the Palestinian Revolution through armed struggle." Passage through Lebanon into Israel was limited to certain areas, and codicils added in May 1970 and accepted by al-Fatah, although not by the PFLP, provided that there would be no firing into Israel from across the Lebanese border or laying of mines and that no Palestinians were to appear in the streets of Lebanon armed.

To those who accepted this agreement, as well as to those who denounced it, the Palestinians' armed presence in Lebanon had now been legitimized. Symbolically, the Arab states that during the Alexandria Conference of 1944, when Lebanon had been accepted as a charter member of the Arab League, had accepted Lebanon's special status and had not asked it to participate in offensive operations against enemies of the Arabs, now expected it to make the necessary sacrifices in the war against Israel. To many rightist Christians the Cairo Agreement was a betrayal of Lebanese sovereignty; to the left it was encouragement to their cause. In effect, the agreement ratified a process that was already well under way, the transformation of the camps into *imperia in imperium*, as they became progressively more heavily armed and impervious to supervision or control by Lebanese security. Lebanese sovereignty correspondingly shrank.

When the Civil War broke out in April 1975, initially the main combatants were the Kata'ib and the Lebanese left. Although officially al-Fatah remained above the fray, it did give some tactical support and arms to the left; the more radical Palestinian groups were more fully involved from the start. At the beginning of 1976, however, after two of its camps were besieged, the Palestinian Resistance Movement (PRM) became fully involved as the principal force against the Lebanese Front. This constituted a victory for the left, by giving them the chance, until Syria decided otherwise, to win a complete victory. As Kamal Joumblatt expressed it in his posthumous *Pour le Liban*, the leftist attempt to seize power was well worth the gamble, even if it ultimately failed.

A question of crucial importance that has often been debated in Lebanon is that of the settlement within Lebanon of many of the Palestinians (numbering 400,000 to 500,000, approximately 14 percent of the total population, in 1982), even should a degree of sovereignty be given them elsewhere, and the effect that such settlement would have on the already threatened sectarian balance. Sixty-five percent were Sunni Muslim; the rest were Christians. After the Civil War, of the 212,000 Palestinians registered on the books of UNRWA, 92,000 were still living in camps, 120,000 outside the camps. About 100,000 of them had been integrated into the Lebanese economy to one degree or another, and 50,000, mostly Christians, had managed to become Lebanese citizens. The figure of 400,000 currently used includes Palestinians who entered the country during and after the first wave in 1948, particularly after 1967 and then in large numbers after Jordan suppressed the Palestinian military presence in that country in 1970–1971.

By 1982, the only Palestinians to remain in areas controlled by the Lebanese Front were in the mainly Christian Dbayya camp. The majority (56 percent of the camp dwellers) were in the south, 23 percent in the north, 13 percent in west Beirut, and 5 percent in the Biqa'. Most of the *fidayeen* (commandos), some 20,000 to 25,000, were in west Beirut and in the south, in an area 35 miles by 6 to 12 miles (59 kilometers by 10 to 20 kilometers) between the Litani and Zahrani rivers. The Palestinians were well armed—in the last months of 1981 they received some $50 million in military equipment from the USSR. And they were well ensconced in some areas with their own schools, shops, clinics, and small industry—what has been called the "Palestine parastate structure."[5] The PLO ran a complex social structure involving most Palestinians in Lebanon; it was a society, in a sense, within a society. Its business and industrial ventures were centralized under SAMED (steadfast in Arabic), it controlled fourteen camps, it ran welfare and medical facilities, and it had a yearly budget of some $400 million. While its political headquarters remained in Damascus, the seat of the National Council, and while technically it had only a political mission in Beirut (under Shafik al-Hout), its leadership was concentrated in Beirut under Arafat, Abu Iyad (Salah Khalaf) as chief deputy, Abud Jihad (Khalil al-Wazir) as chief of staff of the Palestinian Liberation Army (PLA), Farouk Kaddoumi (in charge of foreign affairs), and Hani and Khalid al-Hassan as political advisers. The military establishment included the PLA, allied full-time guerrillas, and auxiliary militia guards (mainly to patrol the camps). Syria, however, controlled two Palestinian brigades (in 1982, one in the north and one in the Biqa') recruited from the 230,000 Palestinian refugees in Syria.

It should be emphasized that many Christians would not be satisifed with the suppression of the Palestinian military force, as occurred in Jordan; they would also insist on the expulsion from the nation of the great majority of these Palestinians to restore the prewar sectarian balance. The solution to the Lebanese problem that has often been proposed—the establishment of a small independent Palestinian state elsewhere—was the only hope, to be sure, but it might not go far enough unless the bulk of the Muslim Palestinians now in Lebanon moved to this new state, or elsewhere. Only then might the revival of the Lebanese polity prove possible.

In 1982, the Lebanese government made a distinction between the Palestinians originally registered with the UNRWA—about 237,000—and the later arrivals. Only the former, many Lebanese felt, should be allowed to remain in Lebanon after the PLO was disarmed. The more intransigent felt that even they should be expelled.

In the traumatic days after June 6, those who suffered the most were civilians, and among these, the Palestinians, especially those in the various camps, were the hardest hit. Camps overrun by the Israelis after heavy bombardment were razed (six by the end of July, including Ain al-Hilweh near Sidon), and at least 20,000 of the refugees were forced, often with no help, to fend for themselves. One reason PLO leaders had insisted on some continuing political presence in Lebanon was to help provide for and help defend these thousands from those who wished them ill, of whom there were many. Among the camp refugees, Israel had planted dragon's teeth.

TWO PORTRAITS: CHAMOUN AND JOUMBLATT

In conclusion to this chapter on polity, portraits of two eminent Lebanese leaders might serve to summarize the events of the republic's turbulent history and offer some further insight. The lives of both Camille Chamoun and Kamal Joumblatt have spanned the history of the Lebanese Republic from its inception through the Civil War. Both figures have been conspicuous on the political scene, both have symbolized important ideals and represented genuine popular impulses, and their lives have been closely intertwined, as friends and then bitter enemies, each the embodiment of one vision or the other of Lebanon's destiny.

The ancestral homes of the Chamouns and of the Joumblatts lie in the Shuf, south of Beirut, the area in which Druzes and Maronites first created the Lebanese entity. The Joumblatts, of Kurdish origin from Aleppo—they came to Lebanon in 1630—were once powerful Druze feudal lords, while the Chamouns, of humbler origin, were among the educated Maronite "scribes" serving these lords for several generations.

Chamoun was born in 1900. In his autobiography he wrote with pride of his hometown, Dayr al-Qamar, capital once of a Lebanon "that the conquests of Fakhr al-Din extended to Aleppo, Damascus and Palestine"; of his father, a functionary of finance in the government of the Mutassarifiate who was exiled during World War I for defying the Turks; and of the awful memory inculcated in him by his elders of the 1860 massacre of hundreds of unarmed Christians in Dayr al-Qamar by the Turks and by the Druzes, over whom, parenthetically, the Joumblatts of the day presided.

Chamoun was educated at a small Catholic school in Dayr al-Qamar, the Pétite Ecole des Soeurs de Saint-Joseph, and the Collège Français du Sacre-Coeur, a prestigious high school in Beirut. In 1920 he entered the School of Law of Saint Joseph. His had thus been a completely French education, typical of many of Lebanon's elite (and quite similar to Joumblatt's). Even while a leading figure in the struggle against the French in the early 1940s, he remained deeply francophile (as did Joumblatt).

After six years practicing law, he began his political career in 1934 when he entered parliament as a deputy from the Shuf, and before the final departure of the French, he served as minister of finance and as minister of the interior (1943–1944). At first a supporter of Emile Iddi, he then joined Bishara Khuri's Constitutional Bloc. He was among the leaders arrested in 1943 by the French, and this fact, in addition to his reputation as a spokesman for the Palestinian and Arab causes at the United Nations, where he served as a representative of Lebanon, and as ambassador to London, gave him the stature to become independent Lebanon's second president.

Chamoun looked the part of president, distinguished in appearance, silver-haired, elegantly dressed, married to a handsome half-English wife. Among the Maronites in particular, he was already becoming, with Gemayel his only competitor, an object of adulation just short of idolatry. In Maronite villages in the 1960s one could find printed icons of him; in one his likeness appeared within a heart upon the bosom of the Virgin Mary, her finger pointing to him with her blessing. During the civil strife of 1958 and after, he was regarded by many Maronites as the embodiment of courage and the "savior of the nation," an opinion he shared.

As president, Chamoun gave free rein to Lebanese capitalism. All limits to free exchange were removed (while the Lebanese pound remained almost completely backed by gold), and Lebanon entered into a period of growing expansion and prosperity after a period of high inflation and unemployment. Women were given the vote. Allegedly to cut down on corruption, the number of electoral districts was reduced from thirty-three to twenty-five and the number of seats in parliament from seventy-seven to forty-four. In foreign affairs, Chamoun saw his chief challenge to be the protection of Lebanon from the threat of "Nasserism" and from Syrian interference. To do this, he sought to strengthen the power of the presidency, and in the process he acted to subvert rather than to exploit and work within the pluralistic system.

One of Chamoun's leading opponents in 1958, once his ally in 1952 when the two had joined in the movement to end the presidency of Bishara Khuri, was Kamal Joumblatt. Joumblatt was born in 1917. He studied first at the Collège des Pères Lazaristes d'Antoura, law at Saint Joseph in Beirut, and then social philosophy at the Sorbonne. In 1942, after the death of the leader of the Joumblatt clan, his uncle Hikmat, he became the nominal leader of this faction of the Druzes, rival since the eighteenth century of the Druze Arslans (the Yazbakis). As patriarch and as patrician, he was a fierce defender of the Druzes, whom he considered to be in many ways the most Arab of the Arabs— speaking the best Arabic, for example. The Druze religion he held to be one that embodied both the rationalism of the Greeks and the mystic and gnostic wisdom of the East, providing the Druzes with a sense of dignity and acceptance.

As well as being something of a mystic, Joumblatt was devoted to socialism, but to a socialism of his own brand, an alloy of Marx, Rousseau, and Gandhi, among others. Government, he believed, should own the major means of production, but small private property should be widely distributed as a basis for genuine democracy; classes existed, but in place of class war he advocated class transcendence; and although violence was sometimes necessary, nonviolence, he believed, was to be preferred. There was always something aloof and withdrawn about Joumblatt, as if the events of the world were predestined or, in any case, of passing significance. For politics as usual, and for politicians, he had complete contempt. His own political posture always seemed ambivalent; he was an Arab nationalist and a Lebanese nationalist, a Marxist and a Jeffersonian of sorts, with sympathy for the USSR, but distaste for its totalitarian features. He was a person of intransigently held principle, yet he cherished Gandhi's statement: "Love of truth has taught me the beauty of compromise!"

Joumblatt first entered politics in 1943 as a deputy from the same constituency as had Chamoun. He had already shown signs of his idealistic fervor in high school when, it is alleged, he briefly became a convert to Christianity; in 1948, when he sold off some of the family land to his sharecroppers; and in 1949, when he founded the Progressive Socialist party (PSP), which reached its peak in 1953 with some 18,000 card-carrying members and some 200 local party committees. In 1952, along with Chamoun, he was a leader of the Socialist National Front that helped to bring Khuri's presidency to an end. By 1958 he had become infamous to the establishment as a dangerous maverick, an uninhibited spokesman against the system, and a relentless gadfly. But both because he represented an important Druze constituency and because he had some clout through his party in the "street," he was co-opted into various ministries. In 1957, now one of Chamoun's fiercest opponents, he was among the leading politicians to be "purged" in the election of 1957 as a result of Chamoun's wily tactics. He became, inevitably, one of the leaders of the opposition in 1958, and his militia was one of the few to engage in serious combat.

In contrast to the elegant Chamoun, Joumblatt dressed his thin, almost haggard, body indifferently. His head jutted forward from hunched shoulders. His lean, almost gaunt, face, with a mustache beneath his hooked nose, gave him an ascetic mien. His eyes reflected intelligence, and his tight mouth suggested a touch of disdain. To his Druze followers he was a hero and the natural hereditary chief; to many of his admirers he was the only establishment leader with a genuine social conscience and a progressive outlook. Michael Hudson, although quite critical of him, credited him with being the first Lebanese leader to arouse a genuine indigenous left-wing spirit.[6] To his enemies he was a combination of a confused and erratic firebrand, an opportunist beneath his moralism, and a charlatan if not a clown, although a dangerous one. In 1958, a current tale had it that he had persuaded an Indian member of the U.N. supervision team (appointed to ensure that no arms entered Lebanon from Syria), while the two stood on their heads in yoga position, that his side had received no assistance from Syria. George Naccache, the columnist and newspaper editor, once described Joumblatt as a part of Lebanon's folklore, an "impresario" who "gives the well-established bourgeoisie the delicious shiver it needs, and without which their taste for the good things of life would begin to fade."[7]

By 1957–1958 Joumblatt had become convinced that Chamoun was, as he indicated in his account of the civil strife (*Haqiqat al-thawra al-lubnaniyya* [Truths about the Lebanese revolt] [1959]), only one more traditional leader with the mentality of a ward-chief rather than that of a statesman, and a hopeless creature of the system, with its sectarianism, corruption, and immobilism. Chamoun was also, in Joumblatt's view, guilty of shady business dealings. Chamoun, in fact, has been closely associated with important businessmen—Emile Bustani, for example, before the latter's death—and he has been on a number of company boards, including the Protein Company, which proposed on the eve of the Civil War in 1975 to modernize Lebanon's ailing fishing industry, only to arouse the fury of Sidon's fishermen and bring Lebanon closer to disaster.

Chamoun, for his part, had become convinced well before 1958 that Joumblatt was "a difficult and sinister person," as he said in his own account of the events of 1958 (*Crise au Moyen-Orient* [Crisis in the Middle East]), fulfilling the warning Sitt Nazira, Joumblatt's mother, who was a political figure of considerable importance in her own right, had given him upon her deathbed. She told Chamoun, according to his own account, that her son was not "normal" and that he needed to be treated with charitable patience. Regarding Joumblatt's socialism, Chamoun was cynical; he observed that once his opponent had flown into a rage when denied a license to build a cement factory in an area that already had one.

The two families of the Shuf, however, in the small theater that Lebanon is, continued to be close. In the events of 1958, when Walid, Kamal's son, was kidnapped, it was Danny, Camille's son, who had him released. Further evidence that 1958, as a whole, was still within the family and hardly the blood-bath 1975 was to become is that Joumblatt, in the thick of battle, continued to receive his mail at his palace in Mukhtara without interruption.

After 1958, when Joumblatt was "in" and Chamoun "out," Chamoun founded a new party, the Party of Free Patriots (Hizb al-Wataniyya al-Ahrar), usually called in English the National Liberal party (NLP), in opposition to President Shihab, whom he perceived to have sold Lebanon down the river to 'Abd al-Nasir and subsequently turned it into a police state. In 1960 the NLP could claim four seats in parliament and in 1964, six—Chamoun, of course, remained a formidable figure on the political scene. In 1968 his party allied with Pierre Gemayel and Raymond Iddi to form the Triple Alliance (Hilf al-Thulathi) to oppose President Hilu, who was attempting to continue the policies of Shihab.

When Franjiyya was elected president in 1970, a victory Chamoun could rightly consider his own, Chamoun served in several ministries, including foreign affairs, and defense. His last post was as minister of the interior under Rashid Karami in 1975. By this time his militia, the Namur (Tigers), had already engaged in combat with the left and with the Palestinians, and while Karami was singlehandedly trying to hold the country together, Chamoun, to the disgruntlement of his opponents, for a period enjoyed the protection and the influence afforded by living in the president's palace. And it was perceived that the commander in chief, General Iskandar Ghanim, to the opposition a symbol of Maronite domination, was Chamoun's creature.

Joumblatt after 1958 continued to lead his PSP, which remained a force in the land. He served in three successive cabinets under President Shihab as minister of the interior. But even while supporting shihabism, he was still the enfant terrible. In 1961, for example, he helped overthrow the government of Sa'b Salam, in whose cabinet he was minister of the interior; then, with the president's support, he resumed this post in the new cabinet of Rashid Karami. In 1969, when asked to enter the government by President Hilu, he posed a number of conditions, most of which in the context of the moment were quite utopian: that obligatory military service be adopted (to fight Israel), full freedom of movement be given to the Palestinians, confessionalism as a basis for elections be abolished, a plan for economic development be undertaken, and industry and agriculture be provided with credit banks. In 1970, while minister of the interior again, after a number of Palestinians were killed while passing through the Christian town of al-Kahalla, he accused his own government of supporting an anti-Palestinian plot in a spirit of intrigue that reminded him of the Costa Gavras movie Z.

In 1970, with Franjiyya's election—when Chamoun was in and Joumblatt out—Joumblatt became increasingly shrill and intransigent in his denunciation of both the government and the system. In October 1973, for example, he accused Sa'b Salam, about to form a government, of being guilty of one crime or another in every ministry he had ever held and of responsibility for persecuting students and for the killing of strikers at the Gandour biscuit factory. After the massacre of April 13, 1975, his pressure to have all pro-Kata'ibi members of the cabinet resign helped in this crucial hour to bring down the government of Rashid Sulh, which he supported. By this time he was already the head of the Lebanese left and of its National Front.

During the Civil War, Joumblatt and Chamoun, of course, were at opposite poles. Chamoun, after the battle of Damour and after his mansion at Sa'diyyat, nearby, had been invaded, plundered, and then razed, moved to the Mountain to continue the struggle as a leading member of the Lebanese Front. Joumblatt, meanwhile, allied with the Palestinians, sought to destroy the established system once and for all, and almost succeeded until the Syrian armed intervention.

Who orchestrated Joumblatt's death in March 1977 may never be known, but it is clear that by this time President Asad of Syria had already decided that Joumblatt was a dangerous nuisance. Joumblatt, for his part, had made clear to Asad that he deplored the Syrian intervention, and he was widely quoted as having said to the Syrian president, "We refuse to become prisoners of Arabism." From Joumblatt's perspective, Asad had been seduced by the United States, acting for Israel, and the rightists, with the illusory chance of recovering prestige in the Arab world and on the international scene by resolving the Lebanese problem and probably with the promise that part or all of Lebanon would be absorbed into Greater Syria. What Asad had now done, Joumblatt believed, was to shatter any hope of transforming Lebanon into a truly nonsectarian progressive state, a model for the whole Arab world.

Responsible together with Syria for the collapse of this revolution of "the third estate and the petite bourgeoisie against the ruling Maronite haute bourgeoisie," as he put it, were both foes and friends. In his *Pour le Liban*, with its sweeping criticism of virtually every person and every community (except the Druze), Joumblatt characterized Maronites as the first Zionists and described them as a talented people but one incapable of rule, a people living in a fossilized past and in an atavistic present. Muslims he saw as having abandoned rationalism after the thirteenth century, as living with the "complex of the Saracen" and with a feeling of inferiority regarding the Maronites. "Progressive" Arab leaders he dismissed as having the mentality of "provincial Ottoman governors" who had defeated the Bismarckian promise of Nasser and feared the example of a just and free Lebanon. And he denounced the ideological rigidity of many of his supporters who unrealistically and irresponsibly had fed Christian "paranoia" and lost potential friends by insisting upon "revolution" and on a sterile type of Marxism hardly relevant, he said, to a society with only about 70,000 industrial workers. Also subject to Joumblatt's disdain were many of his Palestinian allies who, like many of the ideologues, fed Christian fears and helped plunge the nation into tragedy by their oftentimes irresponsible and insolent behavior. His only sympathy was for members of the youth who craved a true nation and fatherland in place of the "false liberalism" they had been fed.

Was only Joumblatt, then, in the right? In fact, the chatelain of Mukhtara was quite capable of regarding himself with wry humor. He admitted to occasional dilettantism and to a feeling of kinship with Don Quixote, and he appreciated the point once made to one of his socialist colleagues (on a mission to seek the support of the Gulf states during the Civil War):

> What's wrong with you people in Lebanon? You preach democracy, but don't you realize that no Arab state wants this at any price? You want the abolition of confessionalist privileges, but almost all the Arab states live according to statutes that are both religious and confessional. You

propose the secularization of laws and institutions, but no one in the region would entertain such a proposition. And with all this, you ask for the political and moral support of the Arab states![8]

Joumblatt, indeed, was an extraordinary man, in many ways unique. Chamoun represented many Lebanese who shared his vision of a liberal, capitalist, laissez-faire, sovereign, and Western-oriented Lebanon; Joumblatt's vision was his own. Lebanon, ultimately, like all worldly constructions, was to him only a speck on the tide of the infinite currents of the cosmos; on the other hand, as some of his critics have maintained, he aspired to create a Lebanon of which he could be president!

One might admire these two very different Lebanese leaders, but one is tempted to conclude that they have both ultimately been failures, Chamoun because of his idealization of the Lebanon that was, Joumblatt because of his idealization of what Lebanon could become.

NOTES

1. David and Audrey Smock, *The Politics of Pluralism: A Comparative Study of Lebanon and Ghana* (New York: Elsevier, 1975); and Iliya F. Harik, "The Political Elite of Lebanon," in George Lenczowski, ed., *Political Elites in the Middle East* (Washington, D.C.: American Enterprise Institute for Public Policy Research, 1975).

2. Malcolm Kerr, "Political Decision Making in a Confessional Democracy," in Leonard Binder, ed., *Politics in Lebanon* (New York: John Wiley, 1966), pp. 187–212.

3. Ibid.

4. Harik, "Political Elite."

5. Rashid Khalidi, quoted in the *Christian Science Monitor*, February 19, 1982.

6. Michael Hudson, *The Precarious Republic: Political Modernization in Lebanon* (New York: Random House, 1968), pp. 183–190.

7. *L'Orient–Le Jour*, June 29, 1971.

8. Kamal Joumblatt, *Pour le Liban* [In behalf of Lebanon] (Paris: Stock, 1978), p. 252.

6

The Collapse of 1975

As anyone knows who has written about Lebanon, particularly Lebanon since 1975, nomenclature presents a problem. Alignments were based only partially upon class, religion, or ideology. This was not a class war, although class conciousness played a role in it; it was not a war of Christian against Muslim, although in terms of numbers on either side this would seem to be true; and it was not a clash simply between left and right, although "leftist" and Marxist predominated on the one side. Even the term "Civil War" itself, some would argue, is a misnomer biased in favor of the view that the Lebanese system had collapsed because of internal flaws rather than because it had been attacked by extrinsic forces.

But terms are necessary to describe what has occurred. Arbitrarily in part, and without prejudging the interpretation of the conflict, the term "Civil War" will be employed because it has gained general currency. The hard-core defenders of an integral Lebanon, a Lebanon rid of Palestinian and, since 1976, Syrian armed forces, and if necessary, the shrinkage of the nation to only the Mountain and part of Beirut, will be designated as "ultras" for want of a better term. The term "nationalist" could not be used, because this would exclude the president and his supporters, who continued to man the legitimate government to which the ultras have often been in opposition. The term "left" will be used to designate extragovernmental forces that have sought a radical transformation of Lebanon into a secular and, to one extent or another, socialist state (even if some groups aligned with them, the various Nasserist elements, for example, have been only superficially socialist). The term "traditional" will be applied to Muslim or Christian leaders who have supported the government and who favored either the retention or only a moderate reconstruction of the *status quo ante bellum.*

The major war goals of the ultras have been to reduce or eliminate the Palestinian presence and, after 1976, to expel the Syrians and to contain if not eliminate the Lebanese left. The war goals of the left

103

have been to revolutionize Lebanese society; the goals of some of the moderate Muslim leaders have been to limit Maronite control of the army and to restructure the system to allow for equal participation of the Muslim community in the system; the goals of most Palestinians have been to protect their bases in Lebanon and to continue to be able to use Lebanon as a springboard for the "liberation of Palestine"; and the goals of radical Palestinians have been to revolutionize Lebanon and other Arab countries and then to combat Israel in the "Vietnamese" style, through a radical mass uprising.

Besides these rational goals, all sorts of visceral as well as self-serving and opportunistic motivations have been in play, among these the desire for revenge, for profit, or simply for the experience of the excitement of war and killing. And in these complicated and troubled waters many fishermen, in Cairo, Baghdad, Damascus, Amman, Tehran, Tripoli, and Jerusalem—and more distantly Washington and Moscow—have cast their various nets. Syria's goal, since 1976, has been to maintain its presence; Israel's goals have been to eliminate this presence, to destroy the PLO as a military and political force, and perhaps to annex southern Lebanon directly or indirectly.

For convenience, the era of Lebanon's travail since 1975 will be divided into four periods: the prelude, going back to at least 1969; the Civil War of 1975–1976, ending with Syria's effective control of much of Lebanon; the period to June 1982, when anarchy was confined to relatively distinct areas and enclaves, with the legitimate government virtually reduced to a shadow; and the period after Israel's massive and brutal invasion on June 6, 1982. The first two periods will be discussed in this chapter, the last two in Chapter 8.

PRELUDE

After a period of relative harmony and prosperity between the resolution of the civil strife of 1958 and the Arab-Israeli war of 1967, matters began to go seriously amiss. The refusal of the army command to involve Lebanese forces in the Six-Day War enraged many Muslim leaders, the progressives, and the Palestinians and fueled existing tensions. The Palestinian armed presence became increasingly visible and, to many Lebanese, increasingly brash and arrogant; in 1969 and 1973 Palestinians clashed with the army, and in 1970 units of the Kata'ib clashed with the Palestinians. Israeli raids became almost routine, by air and land, while the Lebanese government stood helplessly by and saw its legitimacy wane. In December 1968 Israeli commandos landed at the Beirut International Airport and blew up planes of Middle East Airlines; in April 1973 their commandos penetrated Beirut in rented

TABLE 6.1 Main Contenders in the Civil War (by the end of 1976)

Lebanese Front (or Kufur Front) (founded 1976)

Kata'ib (10,000-15,000 core militia; could raise some
   30,000-40,000)
National Liberal party (Chamoun)
Guardians of the Cedar (Etienne Saqir)
Zghartan Liberation Army (the Marada Brigade)(Franjiyya)
Permanent Congress of the Lebanese Orders of Monks
   (Sharbal Qassis)
Al-Tanzim (Fuad Shamali)
"Liberated Lebanon" (Major Sa'd Haddad)(2,000-2,500 forces
   after 1978)
Smaller units

National Movement (FPPNF) (founded 1973)

Progressive Socialist party (Joumblatt family)
Al-Murabitun (Ibrahim Qulailat)
Lebanese Communist party (Georges Hawi)
Arab Socialist Ba'th party (supported by Iraq)
Organization of Communist Action (Muhsin Ibrahim)
Arab Socialist Action party
Syrian Social Nationalist party (In'am Ra'd)
Smaller units
Total: Some 7,000 forces

Allied to the National Movement but Aligned with Syria

Nationalist Front
Organization of the Ba'th party (Asim Qansu)
Union of the Forces of the Working People (Kamal Shatila)
Syrian Social Nationalist party (Ilyas Qanaizah)
Movement of the Disinherited (al-Amal)(Imam Musa al-Sadr;
   then Nabih Berri)

Syrian forces (22,000-30,000)

Lebanese army (25,000 claimed by 1980)

United Nations Interim Force in Lebanon (6,000)

---

cars and killed three prominent Palestinians. The Lebanese army made no effective resistance.

Criticism of the government became increasingly vocal, and the power of traditional leaders began to be seriously challenged. In 1972 'Abd al-Majid al Rafi'i, a pro-Iraqi leftist, and Najah Wakim, a Nasserist, were elected to parliament. In Sidon and environs tobacco growers were objecting to the prices the government monopoly paid for their crops; fishermen, fearing the threatened intrusion into their waters of the modernized fishing company Protein, became increasingly restive and clashed with security forces; and the Shi'ites were becoming increasingly vocal as the Imam al-Sadr organized the new Movement of the Disinherited to challenge the traditional Shi'ite leaders. In February 1975, during a demonstration, Ma'ruf Sa'd, a deputy in parliament and a Nasserist local notable, was shot by security forces. He subsequently died, a martyr to the opposition. Meanwhile, on university campuses and in the streets, students were engaging in one demonstration after another and clashing with the security forces. And both private and party militias were strengthening their muscle with new recruits and weaponry. Lebanon was beginning to break up into a complex of rival feudatories, collectively better armed than the 17,000-man Lebanese army.

By the spring of 1975, it needed only a dramatic incident to set the nation on fire; this incident, as seen, occurred on April 13 when a busload of Palestinians passed through the turf of the Kata'ib party at 'Ayn al-Rummana in southeast Beirut and were fired upon; twenty-seven people were killed. Whether or not this action was justified as retaliation for earlier incidents in which two members of the Kata'ib had been assassinated, the fuse had been ignited.

CIVIL WAR

Accurate and objective accounts of the civil war already exist; perhaps the best to date is Walid Khalidi's *Conflict and Violence in Lebanon: Confrontation in the Middle East* (1979). No effort will be made here to do more than to outline the sequence of events in five parts and to make a number of general comments.

1. *April to September 1975.* Clashes occurred between the militia of the Kata'ib and leftist and Palestinian units and between the inhabitants of 'Ayn al-Rummana (mainly Maronites) and of al-Shiyyah (mainly Shi'ites). The government attempted to impose several cease-fires, but these lasted only briefly. Rashid Karami, at the time the most effective traditional Muslim leader, became prime minister. Camille Chamoun became minister of the interior, and the commander of the army, Iskandar Ghanim, considered to be too ultra, was replaced by Brigadier Hana Sa'id. Syria helped arbitrate a temporary détente in September.

2. *December 1975 to April 1976.* In December 1975 fighting resumed. The ultra National Liberals seized the Palestinian camp of Dbayya, north of Beirut (inhabited mostly by Christian Palestinians); the Palestinians attacked the Christian stronghold of Damour, south of Beirut, after the Kata'ib occupied and destroyed the mainly Muslim areas of the Karantina and al-Maslakh in Beirut. By now the Palestinians, whose

earlier role had been ambiguous, were openly and visibly in the fray, and the ultras were placed increasingly on the defensive. Damour fell on January 20, 1976, and Camille Chamoun's nearby estate was razed. The ultra leader escaped north in a helicopter.

Meanwhile, after consultation with the Syrian government, President Franjiyya issued the Constitutional Document on February 6, 1976, which, it was then hoped, would serve as a basis for the final resolution of the conflict. The document provided for equality of representation in parliament between Muslims and Christians in place of the 6 : 5 formula and for the election by parliament of the prime minister, instead of his being appointed by the president. One purpose of the charter was to isolate the left by winning over most Muslims to the government side. Just at this time, ironically, the army began to disintegrate. Lieutenant Ahmad Khatib led one component to join the National Front under the name the Lebanese Arab Army, and another component, under Colonels Antoine Barakat and Fuad Malik, aligned itself with the ultras; others went home or remained loyal to the central government; and one top officer, Brigadier 'Aziz al-Ahdab, attempted an abortive coup d'état.

In Damascus, President Hafiz Asad was now convinced that should the ultras be finally defeated and the left and the Palestinians acquire predominance in Lebanon, Syria might lose control over the timing of any confrontation with Israel and would be open to an attack through Lebanon. He was also increasingly disturbed lest ripples from a radicalized Lebanon, possibly linked to Iraq, cross over into his country. While publicly in support of the Palestinians, he held them under firm control in Syria and wished to do so in Lebanon as well.

3. *April to May 1976.* Syrian troops entered Lebanon in March as the left and the Palestinians seemed to have victory within their grasp. President Franjiyya's palace outside Beirut was bombed, and he was compelled to flee to the north. Criticism of him was mounting from all quarters, and he was forced to accept a constitutional amendment (to Article 73) passed by parliament setting the date for the election of a new president six rather than three months before the expiration of his term. On May 8, parliament, under gunfire, elected Ilyas Sarkis, the former protégé of Fuad Shihab and the candidate who had almost defeated Franjiyya in 1970, as the new president. The hope was that, even if Franjiyya refused to resign before the expiration of his term, a fresh start might be possible.

4. *June to September 1976.* The Syrians extended and consolidated their hold, and the left and the Palestinian Resistance Movement were brought to heel. The ultras regained control, with Syrian support, of most areas of the Mountain. On September 23, 1976, Sarkis was inaugurated. He appointed a cabinet essentially of "technocraft" under

Selim al-Hoss (and, then in 1980, Shafiq al-Wazzan). Parliament's term
was extended several times, awaiting conditions appropriate for a new
election.

In the broader international context, through the offices of the
United States, it was tacitly agreed that Israel would allow the Syrians
to consolidate their presence, provided they did not cross the "Red
Line," presumably north of the Litani River.

5. *October to November 1976.* Meanwhile, the Arab states, with
Saudi Arabia playing the crucial role, agreed at Riyadh on October 16
to the Syrian presence of some 30,000 troops provided that it was
"Arabized" and included units from other countries. The Syrian troops
were to be the major component of an Arab Deterrent Force (ADF).
Having established their military presence, the Syrians decided to curb
the ultras and defend the left and the Palestinians. By December the
port of Beirut and the airport were functioning regularly again; warfare
was limited to the south. But the Civil War was over only if one limits
the term to the period preceding the establishment of the Arab Deterrent
Force in full control of the most of Lebanon. Violence, terrorism, and
bloodshed continued to take their toll.

Incidents, sometimes bizarre and of minor importance in themselves,
and impromptu remarks of the moment can shed light upon a society's
inner being and, in as complex and often veiled polity such as Lebanon's,
reveal the hidden. Several such incidents and comments during the
Civil War follow:

• In May 1975, President Franjiyya, to shore up order in chaos,
appointed a cabinet of army officers under an aged Muslim brigadier.
Muslim protests were so vociferous—the army being a symbol of
Maronite dominance, the premiership Muslims' chief point of political
influence—that the president was forced to cave in and appoint as
prime minister his traditional enemy, Rashid Karami, a sworn clan
enemy from Muslim Tripoli, the perpetual foe of his own neighboring
Maronite town of Zgharta. Karami proceeded to repeat what he had
said before, that the presidential system had caused Lebanon's ills and
that there was no reason why a Muslim should not be elected president.
Of Camille Chamoun, minister of the interior, as well as leader of one
of the militias involved in the fighting in Beirut, Karami essentially
asked, "Who now will guard the guardians?" ("hamiha haramiha"—
the guard's the thief).

• At the same time—this was before it had become certain that
Lebanon was bound for certain disaster, when humor was still possible—

Beirut street scenes after the Civil War. (Credits: *top*, Milt Fullerton, *Middle East Insight*; *bottom*, Donna Egan)

jokes were made about the fractured French of the francophile Kata'ib commandos, and it was proposed that they be provided with Yves Saint Laurent field glasses, Christian Dior boots, and an Alexander Calder barricade. For their opponents, pearl-inlaid Kalashnikovs were proposed, and journalistic wits were referring to the city of Sidon and environs as the "Arab Republic of Sidon," at a time when Lebanon seemed to be disintegrating into its various components.

• Cease-fires were often broken over minor incidents, reminiscent of confessional strife in the nineteenth century when clashes might begin when a chicken or goat wandered into the wrong yard. In June 1975 a Christian girl was allegedly molested by a Muslim in a Maronite neighborhood of Beirut, and fighting resumed. Similarly, in August 1975 battle resumed after a fight over a pinball machine in Zahlah. (In July 1976, parenthetically, the cease-fire that collapsed was estimated to be the fifty-second.)

• Polls taken in July 1975 by *Monday Morning* (Beirut) showed that Sunnites in Beirut believed the struggle to be between left and right, while most Maronites interviewed saw it as a result of "Arab sabotage." The confusion among observers and actors alike as to what the real issues were was given classic expression by the Melchite archbishop, Grégoire Haddad:

> The battle is between the Palestinians and the Lebanese. No! It is between the Palestinians and the Christians. No! It is between Christians and Muslims. No! It is between Leftists and Rightists. No! It is between Israel and the Palestinians on Lebanese soil. No! It is between international imperialism and Zionism on the one hand, and Lebanon and neighboring states on the other.[1]

And so forth.

• Antagonisms were often expressed by bombing shops and even whole markets. In September 1975 the Muslim bazaar in Martyrs Square was dynamited; in response the mainly Christian Suq al-Tawila was devastated. The real victims were the ordinary people of Beirut.

• While the "battle of the hotels" raged in October and November 1975—involving the luxury edifices of the Saint Georges, the Phoenicia, and the Holiday Inn, among others—in a nearby mainly Muslim quarter, even while clashes between "insiders" and "outsiders" occurred, an American couple teaching at the nearby American University of Beirut lived under the protection and reassurance of their neighbors. They were guests and "insiders." Other fancifully named battles were to include that "of the hospitals" in May 1976, when shells fell on the American University of Beirut hospital and others, and that "of the

A fashionable Beirut bookstore after the Civil War. Note signs in both French and Arabic. (Credit: Donna Egan)

beaches" in June 1981, when sea resorts in Beirut and then in Jounieh, in the Christian north, were hit first by one side, then the other.

• At the same time, the bloody-mindedness that possessed Lebanon revealed itself when, on December 6 ("Black Saturday"), after the discovery of the bodies of four dead Kata'ibis, more than seventy unarmed Muslims were massacred at random. On March 16, when on his way to his residence in Mukhtara, Kamal Joumblatt and his entourage were machine-gunned down; even though the probabilities pointed to Syria as responsible, at least one hundred Christians in the area were massacred by Druzes in retaliation. The spirit of 1860 was always subconsciously there, ready to erupt.

• Refugees from the devastated parts of Beirut who had illegally but understandably occupied many of the beach houses along the Beirut coast were building cinderblock garages on the assumption that when forced to move, they would be more highly compensated in accordance with the law. Lebanese ingenuity even in tragic circumstances was irrepressible: Children equipped themselves with bicycle pumps and offered their services when the police, after the Civil War, tried to curb traffic by letting air out of the tires of illegally parked cars.

• In September 1976 *Time* quoted a Kata'ibi as saying: "I'm fed up with hypocrisy. From now on I'm going to say it publicly and blatantly: I prefer Israelis to Palestinians." And in August the *New York Times* quoted another member of the Kata'ib as saying: "If coexistence with the Muslims means continued mediocrity, we don't want it anymore." Fateful sentiments for any future for Lebanon were the remarks of a young woman in December 1976, when the war appeared to be over, traffic jams had resumed, and the Hotel Vendôme was rapidly being repaired to open for a New Year's gala: "It is depressing. All this has happened and now, first thing, everybody is out as if it had been nothing. It's the attitude. People are happy to be doing the same, stupid things. They don't seem to remember—Lebanon can't ever be the same."[2]

• During and since the Civil War the situation in which the Armenian community of about 200,000 found itself has been peculiar, and uncomfortably so. To the indignation of many ultras, the Armenians, although Christian, have attempted to remain above the fray, and for this they have often been harassed, even threatened, and obliged to pay protection money (to avoid having their shops dynamited). And many Armenians were particularly indignant when in October 1978 a bronze statue near the ultraist town of Bikfaya, erected by them in commemoration of Lebanon's hospitality—the legend read "A token of gratitude to Lebanon, which sheltered us after the Turkish massacre of 1915"—was blown up. During the Civil War, the radical and activist Armenian Secret Army, rather than support any Lebanese side, concentrated on its perennial enemy, the Turks. On December 29, 1975, two rockets were fired at the Turkish Embassy. The army also, at the beginning of that year, bombed the local offices of the World Council of Churches for encouraging migration to the United States and so threatening the community's return one day to its home in eastern Turkey.

Ultras are especially bitter about the Armenians, not only because they have been given haven, but also because they have prospered in Lebanon. Their per capita income has been about $2,740, well above the average, and they own 25 percent of bank savings and deposits and transact 25 percent of the business in Beirut's gold market. The Armenians could point in rebuttal to the considerable contributions they had made to the Lebanese economy and to the fact that in normal times the best-organized Armenian party, the Tashnaq, played an active role in the Lebanese polity and supported the system. Khatchik Babikian, for example, an independent who reflected the Tashnaq line and was allied to Pierre Gemayel, often played an important part in Lebanese political brokerage and served on occasion as a cabinet minister. And in any case, the Armenians might retort, the price of accepting hospitality is hardly expected to involve contributing to the destruction of the host's home.

• Puzzling to many observers of the Lebanese scene has been the provenance of many of the arms that began to flood Lebanon well before and during the Civil War. In a November 24, 1975, *Washington Post* article, Joseph Fitchett disclosed some of the threads. Involved were mysterious arms dealers, among them a Samuel Cummings with possible links to the CIA, who allegedly was supplying the Kata'ib with arms through France, and other dealers who imported arms addressed to the Lebanese Army but clearly destined for other customers. Some arms came from army officers sympathetic to one side or the other. Other arms came from such bizarre sources as Nigeria after the civil war. Names mentioned in this still-mysterious traffic include that of a millionaire Saudi businessman, and it is now clear that many arms for the ultras have been provided by Israel—journalists who witnessed the battle of Tall al-Za'tar claim to have seen equipment with Israeli markings used in the siege. This traffic has also been financed by rich Lebanese emigrants, and by Libya and other Arab states. The full story, when and if it is ever told, will add one more chapter to the intriguing and terrible story of contemporary terrorism.

A 1977 article on Lebanon was appropriately entitled "The War That Won't Go Away,"[3] a situation that persisted into 1982 when the drama of localized anarchy was eclipsed by the fifth Arab-Israeli war, this time between Israel and Syria and the PLO (see Chapter 8). The issues involved in the Civil War, however, still haunted Lebanon and would continue to do so in the years to come. A lugubrious cartoon in August 1982 showed a hooded skeleton on a television screen announcing over a Lebanese station, ". . . And now we return to our regularly scheduled Civil War."[4] One could only hope that the announcement was not prophetic.

RETROSPECT

There are a number of questions that one might ask regarding the Lebanese Civil War, even if answers to them can be only tentative and speculative. Was the Lebanese system bound to collapse? Was the collapse fundamentally a result of ethnicity? Religion? Class? Or was it of foreign and extrinsic provenance? And finally, what are the options for the future? Questions such as these have obvious importance for the Lebanese themselves; and they also have some relevance to the contemporary human condition.

Several reasons may be advanced for the collapse of 1975. First, Lebanon had failed to develop an inner nucleus of sufficient extent to hold in orbit incompatible contending ideological and sectarian interests and ideals. Under pressure, centrifugal forces proved stronger than centripetal ones: Legitimization, loyalty to the whole, and consensus were outweighed by identifications that have been extranational as well as localist and communal; and even where loyalty existed, it tended to be abrasive and exclusivist in many respects and served to exacerbate opposition rather than to absorb and assimilate it. This tendency was only made the more dangerous by the creation of Greater Lebanon in 1920, which fed the pride of Lebanese nationalists but brought into their territory many Muslims whose loyalty and whose identification were to "Syria" and to a larger Arab nation rather than to Lebanon. Even if in times of prosperity there was a degree of consensus, grounded in common vested interest if nothing else, this consensus was negative; it was based too much upon agreement as to what to avoid, not what to accomplish in common. And even if prosperity was greater in Lebanon than in neighboring Arab countries, it was unevenly distributed among regions, classes, and communities. Clearly, to enjoy a less tenuous viability in the future much would need to be done to increase equality of political participation, to make social investment more equitable, and as important as these, to fashion (through a less heterogeneous educational system, for example) a common *and* a positive sense of identity.

Second, because of the absence of an inner core, extrinsic factors beyond Lebanon's own control, such as world inflation and rivalries between the powers, between Israel and the Arabs, and between Arab states, made Lebanon more than normally vulnerable. This had been the situation in the past when external powers both encouraged internal divisions by setting one faction against another and so helped to produce collapse, then reestablished some stability by intervention, as in 1841–1842, 1861, and 1958. One might conclude that Lebanon, hostage in this way to the vagaries of international politics, can prove viable only if and when the powers decide that Lebanon's stability is more important to them than its destabilization. There are good reasons for the powers to adopt the second course. Lebanon can be useful, perhaps uniquely so, as a forum, as a center for international financial and commercial intercourse—and this between incompatible social systems—and as an experiment in multiethnic coexistence.

But even should this international problem ever be resolved, this will be only a condition for the solution of Lebanon's own problems, not in itself a resolution of them. The Lebanese themselves need to confront and to answer the question of what the intrinsic reasons were for the collapse of 1975—and not, as some are prone to do, to simply take the facile approach of blaming others exclusively for their woes. Extrinsic reasons, to be sure, are of crucial importance, and fate has been unkind to Lebanon, but others have overcome extreme adversity, and no nation can hope to survive on international sympathy alone.

Clearly, economic, social, and ethnic factors have all played an important role in preventing Lebanon from becoming a viable and cohesive national entity. In a way, the argument among diagnosticians as to whether the primordial or the class identification is the crucial factor smacks of the chicken and the egg. Each has reinforced the other. The behavior of many Shi'ites, for example, can be understood only in terms of both their relative poverty and their frustration as a community; and it will not do, as some class analysts have suggested, to dismiss the ultraist loyalty of the lower levels of the Maronite community as simply a case of "false consciousness," even if they have been, on the average, better off than their Muslim counterparts. At the higher levels, prosperous Muslim leaders who have sent their children to private French schools, have had business partnerships with Maronite colleagues, and so forth may have often supported extra-Lebanese causes for tactical reasons—to keep the support of their clientele, for example, and counter the appeal of social radicals—but they have done so also because of their genuine belief that Lebanon must participate more positively in the Arab movement, and that Islam must be given a more respectable status in any independent Lebanon.

One might also ask, how could one extricate the social and economic from the sectarian factors in the incidents preceding the Civil War? For example, in March 1975, fishermen, among others, threatened in their livelihood, demonstrated against an army they perceived to represent the Christian establishment, and Rashid Sulh, prime minister at the time, could state, "If the Lebanese army is the army of the Christians, the Palestinians are the army of the Muslims."[5] And in fact, rich and poor, Christians and Muslims, fought on either side in the Civil War— points of view, not religion or income as such, determined alignments. Even a student like Halim Barakat, whose approach tends to be Marxist, recognized this when he concluded: "The most reliable method of classifying the participants in the Lebanese civil war, then, is not by religion or class but by the division between those who seek basic and comprehensive change from those who would maintain the status quo."[6] Any internal resolution of Lebanon's problems, in short, must be based upon addressing social and sectarian issues simultaneously.

Given Lebanon's unstable and problem-ridden society and the perilous international context, one might return to the question raised earlier as to whether extrinsic or intrinsic factors were responsible for Lebanon's collapse. To put it in a different way, was disintegration inevitable because of internal vulnerability or because of an unfavorable international situation that made it impossible for Lebanon to solve its own problems, problems that given the chance, the Lebanese could have resolved through their own institutions and traditions?

Although such a question may never be answered to anyone's full satisfaction, it is worth considering because of the implications any answer has for the future, for the manner in which the reconstruction of the nation is conducted, and even for the desirability or likelihood of any such reconstruction. Students of Lebanon, equally lucid and using the same data, have differed over their answers, whether they have written with the advantage of hindsight or whether they wrote before the Civil War. Failure to predict the war, one might suggest, is not necessarily evidence of faulty analysis, unless one adopts an easy inevitabilitarian view of history. One might, for example, have taken the view that Lebanon was institutionally able to confront its own problems but was never given the chance because of the Palestinian problem and because of Lebanon's unwilling and fateful absorption into this problem.

Scholars who without benefit of hindsight viewed the Lebanese scene pessimistically include Michael Hudson and Halim Barakat. Hudson's main thesis in his *The Precarious Republic* (1968) was that with rapid social modernization Lebanon failed to develop the institutions necessary to bear the load of rising expectations. He quoted Samuel Huntington to the effect that "the non-Western countries of today can have political modernization or they can have democratic pluralism; but they cannot normally have both."[7] Hudson later indicated that he felt events had confirmed his diagnosis.[8]

Elie Salem, on the other hand, in his unfortunately entitled *Modernization Without Revolution: Lebanon's Experience* (1973), basing his argument in part on the Shihab reform movement, proposed that Lebanon could, through its own effort, modernize its administrative system and provide for greater social and economic justice and equity. This was also the point of view of Iliya Harik, who maintained that Lebanon was a viable democracy, that in normal times leaders of the different sects had more in common than not, and that the constitutional system, by providing, for example, that elections were conducted on an intrasectarian and not an intersectarian basis, did constitute a ground for intercommunitarian cooperation.[9] He further argued that the alternative to democratic sectarianism in the Middle East, with its mosaic society and primoridal identifications, could only be the ideological authoritarianism adopted by most of the other Arab nations.

Writing with hindsight, but in fact only repeating what he had maintained before the collapse, Halim Barakat rejected such an optimistic analysis. Because of the lack of any consensus, the growing gap between rich and poor, government corruption and inefficiency, and its rigid sectarian structure, Lebanon was unable to reform itself (the Shihab reform, for example, according to Barakat, amounted to little and in no way adapted Lebanon's irresponsible laissez-faire system to the need for social transformation and for social justice). Lebanon, he implied, was condemned to disintegration and could be saved only by a radical revolution.[10]

But in this devastating picture of Lebanon, Barakat, in distinguishing between "causal" or essential reasons for the collapse and "contributing" or contingent reasons (the Palestine presence, Israeli raids, etc.), seemed to beg the question. The question as to what were the essential and what were the contingent factors accounting for Lebanon's disintegration, while unanswerable, is not a matter of semantics alone. It is a matter of judgment, of faith and determination, and of philosophy. Ultimately, it is a matter of choice and of gambling on the future. The present writer would gamble on the democratic and pluralistic solution; he would give at least one cheer for the Lebanese Republic as it existed before the early 1970s; and while he would agree to the existence of many of the weaknesses of the system Barakat pointed to, he does not share the latter's wholly negative view of the Lebanon that was or might again be.

One interpretation of the Civil War that remains to be considered—one that may be important only because it is believed by many, not because it is objectively persuasive—is that the Civil War was stage-managed, a result of one plot or another. One version of this plot theory is that the Civil War was orchestrated by the ultras in league with the United States—through the CIA, of course—and Israel, to crush the PLO once and for all and in the process neutralize the Lebanese left. Kamal Joumblatt, in his posthumous *Pour le Liban* (1978), subscribed to this interpretation. Another version of the plot theory, one held by some ultras, is that the war was orchestrated by the left in alliance with the Palestinians and supported by radical states such as Iraq, Libya, and Syria, with the Soviet Union's blessing, to seize power in Lebanon, destory Lebanon as a system, use it as a base against Israel, and eliminate the U.S. presence in the area. Future historians, to be sure, on the basis of knowledge not now available, may give credence to either of these myths tomorrow, improbably reductive as they might seem today, when belief in them can only serve to discourage self-examination, compromise, and dialogue.

NOTES

1. Quoted in Trudy Rubin, "Christians, Muslims and Fanatics," *New Republic*, October 25, 1975, pp. 12–15.

2. Quoted in *International Herald Tribune,* November 18, 1976.

3. James Markham, *New York Times Magazine,* October 9, 1977.

4. *Dayton Journal Herald,* August 31, 1982.

5. Nadine Picaudou, *Le Monde Diplomatique,* May 1981, p. 6.

6. Halim Barakat, "The Social Context," in P. Edward Haley and Lewis W. Snider, eds., *Lebanon in Crisis: Participants and Issues* (Syracuse, N.Y.: Syracuse University Press, 1979), pp. 1–20.

7. Samuel Huntington, "Political Modernization: America vs. Europe," *World Politics,* April 1966, p. 412, quoted in Michael Hudson, *The Precarious Republic: Political Modernization in Lebanon* (New York: Random House, 1968), p. 13.

8. Michael Hudson, *Arab Politics: The Search for Legitimacy* (New Haven, Conn.: Yale University Press, 1977).

9. Iliya Harik, "The Ethnic Revolution and Political Integration in the Middle East," *International Journal of Middle East Affairs,* July 1972, pp. 303–323.

10. Barakat, "Social Context."

7

Interlude: 1976–1982

Israel's invasion of Lebanon in the summer of 1982 constituted a watershed. Between the formal, if not real, ending of the Civil War in 1976 and the invasion, there ensued a period of six years, with characteristics of its own that set the stage for Israel's dramatic onslaught. From the vantage point of 1982, this period constituted only a brief interlude in Lebanon's travail, but one whose developments could be of considerable relevance to the future.

A feature of this period was the de facto division of Lebanon into discrete units, with violence within and between these units an everyday occurrence, to be sure, but with enough continuity in some cases to warrant concern over the future of Lebanon. Prior to this the nation had been in jeopardy enough, but now the possibility existed that Lebanon, at least Greater Lebanon, might never be restored. On the other hand, in spite of the extreme fragmentation of Lebanese sovereignty, the Lebanese, in general, continued to support the legitimacy of the traditional structure, and the survival of this structure, if only symbolically, meant that the disintegration of the republic was never complete or irrevocable.

FRAGMENTATION

The crazy-quilt nature of Lebanon had become particularly marked by 1978, after the invasion of south Lebanon by the Israeli army in order to move against the Palestinians and the creation of the autonomous border region under the control of Major Sa'd Haddad. This was a thin region increasingly integrated into Israel by road and electricity networks and by a regular supply of Israeli military equipment, even uniforms. Patches of this quilt were controlled by some 90 individual armed groups (although one observer claims to have counted 164). The legitimate government of Ilyas Sarkis, which in theory ruled the whole nation,

LEBANON, JUNE 1982

SYRIA

• Halba
□ Nahr al-Barid
□ al-Baddawi

Tripoli

• Zgharta

① ADF (Syrians)

• Ihdin

al-Batrun • KURA
CEDARS

MEDITERRANEAN SEA

Byblos

KISRWAN
Baalbeck
• BIQA
Jounieh
② Wavell

BEIRUT • Dhour El Shwyr

Burj
al-Barajnah
• Zahiab

Damour
SYRIA

SHUF

Sidon
□ Ain al-Hulwa Rashayya
□ al-Miyya • "Red Line"

③ • DAMASCUS
Nabatiyya ④
Litani R. □ ⑤

Tyre • Burj GOLAN
al-Rashidiyya □ □ al
Shimali

Bint
Jbeil

ISRAEL

① ADF (Syrians)

② Lebanese Front

③ PLO

④ UNIFIL

⑤ Rightist Controlled Zone
Also called Israel's "Security Belt"

□ Palestinian Refugee Camp

• Town or Village

BEIRUT & ENVIRONS

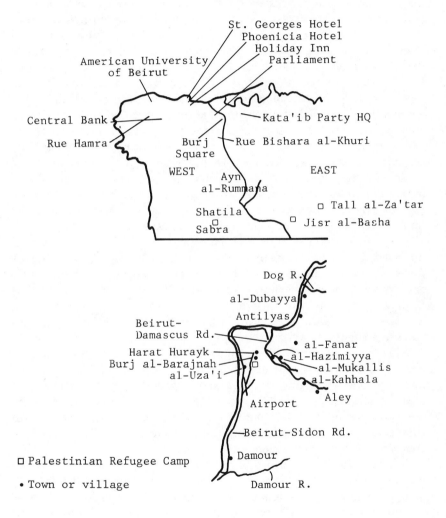

St. Georges Hotel
Phoenicia Hotel
Holiday Inn
Parliament

American University
of Beirut

Central Bank

Rue Hamra

Kata'ib Party HQ

Burj
Square

Rue Bishara al-Khuri

WEST

Ayn
al-Rummana

EAST

Shatila

Sabra

Tall al-Za'tar

Jisr al-Basha

Dog R.

al-Dubayya

Antilyas

Beirut-
Damascus Rd.

al-Fanar

Harat Hurayk
Burj al-Barajnah
al-Uza'i

al-Hazimiyya
al-Mukallis
al-Kahhala

Aley

Airport

Beirut-Sidon Rd.

□ Palestinian Refugee Camp

Damour

• Town or village

Damour R.

in fact controlled practically none of it, in spite of efforts to position units of the newly constituted Lebanese army in strategic spots.

Within and between the various segments into which Lebanon had been fragmented, frequent clashes occurred—between the Syrians and units of the reconstituted Lebanese army in February 1978, for example, and between the Syrians and the ultras in July, when the mainly Maronite part of eastern Beirut, Ashrafiyyah, was heavily bombed and many residents were forced to seek refuge in the north. The ultras, who had once welcomed the intervention of the Syrians, now demanded their withdrawal. Syria's strategy appeared to be to employ force against the ultras, as it had earlier against the Palestinians, only when the former sought to expand beyond their base. Syria's intent has been to divide in order to dominate. Arab opinion would never allow the elimination of the Palestinians, and the ultras, even allied to the Israeli enemy, were needed by Syria as a counter to the Palestinians. In March 1981, units of the Kata'ib began to build a road, apparently to facilitate communication between their northern and southern positions; the battle of Zahlah broke out when the Syrians, fearing a threat to their communication lines with the Biqa', besieged this mainly Greek Catholic city. In July the Syrians ended their siege when it was arranged for units of the Lebanese army to replace the Kata'ib.

Meanwhile the war between Israel and the Palestinians continued unabated. The victims were mainly the Shi'ites, who fled by the hundreds to Beirut and elsewhere, and Lebanese and Palestinians in the cities and towns where Palestinian commandos had bases. This conflict continued into July 1981 when, after the ruthless Israeli bombing of the Fakahani district of Beirut (close to Shatila, one of the largest Palestinian refugee camps), world opinion and U.S. pressure helped to provide for a cease-fire. In return for Israel's ceasing its air raids, the Palestinians agreed to silence their multiple-barrel Katyushas, which had rained rockets onto Nahariya and Qiryat Shemona in Israel. The most spectacular event in this struggle was the invasion in force by the Israeli army into the south in March 1978, after the Palestinian commandos had launched an attack inside Israel and killed thirty-four civilians and wounded seventy-eight others.

To obtain the departure of the Israeli army, the U.N. established the 6,000-man United Nations Interim Force in Lebanon (UNIFIL) to attempt to stop the Palestinians from crossing into Israel with impunity, pending the arrival of the reconstituted Lebanese army. Intended to be a purely defensive mission and armed accordingly, UNIFIL was indifferently successful in curbing the Palestinians, and members of the different national units (Irish, Nigerian, Senegalese, Fijian, Dutch, and Ghanaian) suffered frequent casualties. When they departed, the Israelis

Palestinian guerrillas. *Above:* Note extreme youth of these fighters; *left:* PLO combatant looking out over Israel from Beaufort Castle. (Credit: Mark Lane)

set up the maverick Christian officer, Major Sa'd Haddad, in charge of the area bordering Israel. In July 1979, Haddad proclaimed this area "independent free Lebanon."

The Palestinian-Israeli conflict often brought Syria and Israel to the verge of open confrontation. This was particularly true in 1981 when Israel, claiming that the Syrians were "massacring the Christians" in Zahlah, shot down two Syrian helicopters. Syria responded by installing several SAM-6 missile launchers in the central Biqa' and proceeded to shoot down a number of Israeli unmanned planes with them. The ongoing U.S. peace mission of Philip Habib, as well as the special Arab League peacemaking commission (composed of the foreign ministers of Saudi Arabia, Kuwait, and Syria and sponsored by the Arab League), was placed in an embarrassing position, and war between Syria and Israel threatened when the Syrians refused the Israeli demand that the missile launchers be removed. Surprisingly, instead of attending to their removal, Israel launched an attack on Iraq's nuclear plant near Baghdad on June 7, and the crisis of the missile launchers was over-shadowed. But Israel continued to bomb Palestinian bases along the coast, as seen, although avoiding exposure to the SAM-6's, and on July 17 made the massive attack on part of Beirut.

Violence also continued among the Lebanese themselves, and even intramurally, among the Maronites. The National Movement, the grouping of leftist Lebanese parties, suffered a serious setback when on March 16, 1977, Kamal Joumblatt was assassinated. And clashes occurred between units of the Shi'ite al-Amal militia and the pro-Iraqi leftists, reflecting in part the revolution in 1978 in Iran and the subsequent war between Iran and Iraq.

Among the ultras themselves, the unifying thread in the violent confrontations that occurred was the ambition of Bashir Gemayel, already chosen to be the unified military commander of the Lebanese Front, to consolidate Kata'ib control of all the levers of power in the Mountain. In July 1978, units of the Kata'ib had murdered Tony Franjiyya (and his wife and entourage), the son of the ex-president and the commander of the so-called Mardaites, a militia named after Byzantine border guards in charge of defending northern Lebanon from the Muslims in the fourteenth and fifteenth centuries. This led to the disaffection of the Franjiyya clan and the strengthening of ties they already had with the Syrians. On July 7, 1980, Bashir Gemayel struck at the largest ultra force after his own, the militia of Camille Chamoun's National Liberal party, and forced it into submission, even with the disapproval of his own brother, Amin.

Lebanese also killed one another in the bizarre affair known as the "battle of the beaches," which spread terror along Beirut's beaches and killed eight and wounded many more. On June 3 both sides agreed to desist from such attacks to concentrate upon more important matters.

While anarchy continued to hold sway within more or less fixed borders, there were certain important developments between 1976 and June 1982, fateful for the future of the country, that deserve comment.

On the international scene, while the United States seemed to prove through the 1979 and 1981 missions of Philip Habib that it was intent upon a deténte in Lebanon and even a solution to the Lebanese imbroglio, friends and foes alike in the area complained that nothing could even begin to be resolved until the United States negotiated directly with the PLO and pressured Israel to do the same. The Camp David Agreement was generally seen as a failure; many considered Anwar Sadat as something of a traitor; and there seemed to be no real prospect that Israel intended to curb its ambitions on the occupied West Bank or ever to accept the prospect of any real autonomy, let alone independence, for the Palestinians. The USSR was, in the summer of 1981, gingerly making some headway toward retrieving the influence in the area that it had been steadily losing; the assistance pact in October 1980 with Syria was at least a symbolic counter to Israel. In the kaleidoscope of the Middle East, of course, all this could change overnight. Most students of the area, as well as journalists, had by now accepted as a cliché, but a valid one, that the only hope for Lebanon was the creation of some sort of state into which the armed Palestinian presence could be moved. Only then would there be a logical and a convincing basis for the departure of the Syrians and for giving the Lebanese a chance to try to mend their own fences.

In the meantime, the damage to Lebanon was bound to leave grim scars and, perhaps even more dangerous, haunting memories for the future. Damage included the some 30,000 to 40,000 killed during the Civil War (the precise figure is a moot point among scholars), the $5 billion worth of physical damage, the 300,000 refugees from the south who needed to be resettled or assimilated, the dangers inherent in having raised the "Kalashnikov generation" that knows little more than the violence and crime of the street, and the aggravation of sectarian hostilities. In the south damage between 1978 and the spring of 1981 included the following: 3,000 families lost their breadwinners; 8,000 people were handicapped, 11,000 were orphaned, 5,000 wounded, and 1,000 killed; 9,400 buildings were destroyed and 21,500 heavily damaged; the four largest towns of Bint Jbail, Tyre, Nabatiyya, and Khiyam had become ghost towns; 11,000 dunums (a dunum is 1,000 square meters, or approximately one-quarter of an acre) of tobacco were destroyed, 51,000 olive trees, and 70,000 fruit trees; and 3,000 dunums of agricultural land had to be abandoned because of mines.[1]

TABLE 7.1   Chronological Landmarks Since 1976

1977

March 16   Assassination of Kamal Joumblatt
July   Shtaura Agreement between Sarkis, Syria, and the
   Palestinians reviving the Cairo Agreement of 1969

1978

February   Clashes between Syrians and units of the
   Lebanese army
March 15   After 34 Israelis killed, 78 wounded, Israeli
   army invades the south
April-May   Withdrawal of Israeli troops and creation of
   the security border belt under Sa'd Haddad; UNIFIL
   forces arrive
July   Syrians heavily bomb Ashraffiyah, Christian section
   of east Beirut

1979

April   In one of Israel's many air raids into Lebanon,
   more than 100 casualties

1980

March 7   Syrians withdraw from Christian areas of Beirut
October-May   Five penetrations of Lebanon by Israeli
   forces
July 7   Kata'ib under Bashir Gemayel crushes the forces of
   Camille Chamoun's National Liberal party
October   Syrian-Russian Assistance Pact signed

1981

March   Kata'ib begins to construct a strategic road at
   Zahlah
April   Battle of Zahlah begins
April 28   Israel shoots down two Syrian helicopters
April 29   Syria moves SAM missiles into the central Biqa'
June 7   Israeli planes destroy Iraqi nuclear plant
June 30   Begin emerges shaky victor of Israeli elections
July 1   End of the Battle of Zahlah; the Kata'ib withdraws
July 10   Israel resumes heavy bombing in Lebanon
July 15   Palestinians fire rockets at Israeli settlements
July 17   Several hundreds killed, many more wounded, in
   Israeli bombardment of Beirut
July 24   Through the offices of Philip Habib, Saudi
   Arabia, and the U.N., a truce arranged between the
   PLO and Israel (indirectly) to cease mutual attacks
   across Lebanon's border

1982

June 3   Israeli ambassador in London shot
June 6   Israel invades Lebanon
June 14   West Beirut fully encircled by Israel and Kata'ib
August 18   Lebanese government officially asks for the
   withdrawal of the PLO and the mission to Lebanon of
   the multinational force (French, Italians, Americans)
August 19   Israeli cabinet accepts the withdrawal plan
   negotiated by Philip Habib
August 21   Evacuation of the PLO from west Beirut begins
August 23   Bashir Gemayel elected president of Lebanon (to
   assume office September 23)
September 14   Assassination of Bashir Gemayel
September 23   Inauguration of Amin Gemayel as president

Phalangists in Damour, 1982. (Credit: *Middle East Insight*)

Representative of the Lebanese tragedy was the beleaguered town
of Damour, "a nightmare image," as a Quaker observer, James Fine,
described it in 1981. In the Civil War this mainly Christian community,
the headquarters of Camille Chamoun, was attacked and looted by
Palestinian units. Subsequently, as a Palestinian base, it was frequently
bombed by Israel. In 1982 it remained marked by bomb craters, destroyed
houses, and empty lots. It consisted of three distinct neighborhoods,
one of Palestinian refugees from Tall al-Za'tar, the armed camp captured
and razed by the Kata'ib in August 1976 after a relentless siege. The
second quarter was inhabited by Muslim Lebanese refugees from the
occupation and destruction of the Karantina quarter of Beirut in the
earlier stages of the Civil War. And the third quarter was inhabited by
some of the original Christian inhabitants, allowed to stay as a token
to prove that the Palestinian struggle was nonsectarian. Southwest of
Damour was the Palestinian encampment from which commandos left
on the mission that led to the massacre of about thirty-seven Israelis
and the retaliatory invasion of the south in March 1978.

Damour's travail continued. During the Israeli sweep in June 1982,
the Palestinian residents fled, leaving "a mournful ghost town."[2] "The
Israeli onslaught had destroyed almost every house and apartment block,
leaving the air filled with the stench of rotting corpses and trickling

columns of smoke. The only signs of life were a few scavenging dogs and an old, white-haired Lebanese woman."³ As though a cycle had now been completed, some of the original Christian residents returned to pick up the pieces of their lives.

Another development important for the future was the new activism and sense of purpose among the Shi'ite community, the "lowest man" to date on the Lebanese totem pole. On the eve of the Civil War, the Imam Musa al-Sadr had established the Movement of the Disinherited and the organization al-Amal (Hope) to challenge the traditional large-landholding Shi'ite leaders of the day and to defend the interests of his community. Following his mysterious disappearance in 1978, leadership of al-Amal was taken over by Nabih Berri, who has developed it into an effective and well-armed fighting force, quite capable of defending Shi'ite turf. In 1981 it clashed with the Palestine Arab Liberation Front (ALF), which at the time was aligned with Iraq, the enemy of Shi'ite Iran, and in August 1981 with the Lebanese Communists over turf and clientele in the lower-income areas of Shayyah and Bourj al-Barajna; on the sixteenth and seventeenth twenty were killed and sixty-eight wounded. On January 6, 1982, a three-day battle between al-Amal and the Organization of Communist Action (OCAL) ended with seventeen dead and forty wounded. In December 1981 and February 1982 Shi'ites demonstrated to demand the return of their leader, the Imam Sadr, who had disappeared in Libya in August 1978, by hijacking two airplanes. Posters with Sadr's likeness covered walls in the Basta and Patriarchate districts of Beirut, previously Sunnite strongholds.

Where the Shi'ites would throw their weight was uncertain; they were nominally associated with the National Movement, but the ultras hoped that the Shi'ites could be tempted to join them to help weigh down the balance against hostile Sunnite traditional leaders, the left, and the Palestinians. This hope was based upon reports of growing Shi'ite disenchantment with the Palestinian cause, which had brought so much suffering to the Shi'ite community by encouraging Israeli reprisal and preemptive raids into the south. Many Shi'ites had also become indignant over the behavior of certain Palestinian elements in Tyre and elsewhere, who lorded it over them and extorted protection money.

Shi'ites were now well aware that they constituted the largest Muslim confession, and they were and remain unlikely to submit to Sunnite predominance any longer; some even believe, now that they outnumber any single Christian sect, that the presidency might some day be theirs. An unusual factor involved in the Shi'ites' behavior was the understanding that they came to in 1973 with the Syrian leadership, which is principally Alawite, that the Alawite faith can be considered to be a version of Shi'ite orthodoxy. Lebanese Mitawalis (Shi'ites) and Syrian Alawites, the implication was, have a common interest in sticking together in a part of the Middle East in which the Sunnites have an overwhelming majority. On the Lebanese chessboard, the Syrians hoped that the Shi'ites could serve to help keep the PLO in check. Adding to this intricate maze was the fact that the Palestinians confronted the dilemma of whether to support Iraq and so antagonize the Shi'ites or to support the Iranian revolution and its defensive war against Iraq and so lose the support of other Arabs. Al-Amal, by 1982, had a militia of 4,000 to 5,000. While steadfast in the defense of the Shi'ite community, however, it was not a cohesive bloc, as was the Kata'ib. It represented various, often incompatible tendencies, ranging from the secular reformist to the pro-Iranian and pro-Khomeini and including those close to Damascus, to the PLO, to the Lebanese Front, and to the traditional and conservative leadership. During the Israeli invasion, while southern Shi'ites appeared to be solidly hostile to the PLO and to cooperate with Major Haddad, in the north elements of the Shi'ite community joined Palestinians in resistance to the Israeli army. Shi'ites did have in common, nevertheless, a determination that they would in the future play a role commensurate with their numbers and no longer continue to be the whipping boy in the Lebanese system.

A final development to be considered was the progressive con-solidation of what amounted to virtually a separate nation in the territory controlled by the ultras, an area of some 800 square miles (2,000 square kilometers), 20 percent of Greater Lebanon. There has always been, as discussed earlier, a strong separatist ethnic sense among the Maronites, one encouraged by the church. To the ultra die-hards, Lebanon, whatever its future might be, must remain a state controlled by Christians, a haven, or island, in the sea of Muslims around it. In 1947, Maronite Archbishop Mubarak proposed the creation of a separate Christian state to parallel the creation of a Jewish state in Palestine. Today the leading Maronite poet and ideologue, Sa'id 'Aql, continues to argue that the Maronites are of Phoenician and not Arab descent, that classical Arabic is a dead language, and that Lebanese children should be taught Western languages and their own colloquial Lebanese dialect of Arabic. The Kata'ib, founded as the shield of the Maronite identification, since 1975 has returned to its original intransigent position of 1936, when it was founded, and abandoned the pragmatic moderation it exhibited in calmer days when, for example, it could support President Shihab's reformism and his effort to reconcile Lebanon with the other Arab nations.

Fortunately, however, for any possible future for Greater Lebanon, the patriarch, Antonius Pierre Khuraysh continued unobtrusively to urge reconciliation among the various Lebanese factions, and many Greek

Catholics have been reluctant to give the ultras their full support. Even within the Kata'ib party, Amin Gemayel was critical of his brother; and Danny Chamoun, son of Camille, and other elements of the National Liberal party, remained disaffected from Bashir Gemayel. And a leading Kata'ib ideologue and politburo member, Karim Pakradouni, once indicated unhappiness over the close connection with Israel that the Kata'ib has maintained since 1975. In an August 8, 1978, article in *Le Monde*, he had warned that the two errors to be avoided were, one, to assume that the Syrians could be or even needed to be evicted by force and, two, to ally with Israel and risk becoming an Israeli "kibbutz," something probably not even the Israelis wanted. The thesis he propounded was *"libanisation,"* divorcing Lebanon from Arab or Islamic traits and restoring links with a Phoenician past—a position not very different from that of President Sarkis.

And the Kata'ib has also been opposed by the remains of Iddi's National Bloc, by the Franjiyya clan with its Mardaite militia, and by many Greek Orthodox led by the Syrian Social Nationalist party, which continued to be a factor, holding out into 1982, as in the town of Dour Schweir.

Nevertheless, the Mountain has been well on its way toward being molded into a separate entity. The ultra community, with its capital in Jounieh, has developed its own administrative structures, united army, and policy; provided for the collection of taxes; and built its own seaport and airport. Jounieh has become a prosperous and expanding small metropolis. In 1977, whether for purely tactical reasons or not, both Camille Chamoun and Pierre Gemayel declared that the National Pact was dead, and in their entourage the question was discussed whether the formation in 1920 of Greater Lebanon had not been a grievous error. In 1978 the leaders of the politburo of the Lebanese Front rejected President Sarkis's plea for all militia groups to lay down their arms and even opposed the re-creation of a Lebanese army. During and since the Civil War, the ultras have not hesitated to accept arms and advice from Israel, at first clandestinely and since 1976 openly and defiantly, although in the summer of 1981 there were indications they might compromise and abandon this alliance, and in June 1982 they did not join the invading Israelis—at least not militarily.

The ideological center of the ultra entity has become the University of the Holy Spirit in Kaslik (which is also the site of a fashionable yachting club). Established in reaction to the founding in 1960 of the Egyptian-sponsored Arab University of Beirut, it was originally oriented mainly toward theology but evolved into a regular university. The ideological emphasis has been upon *"Phénicité,"* *"Libanité,"* and *"Ma-*

ronité"; the subjects concentrated upon have been the history of the Maronites, Arabic literature written by Christians, and the like.

Even opponents of the ultras who have considered them fascists have agreed that their entity has been efficiently and strictly run. Garbage has been regularly collected, order has been kept in the streets, and the list of prices of commodity goods have been announced daily on the radio; offenders have been severely punished.

The ultra entity, however, retained important economic links with the rest of Lebanon; many residents still crossed into west Beirut, across the Green Line separating it from east Beirut, to work; some 60 percent of the companies created in Lebanon in 1979 had both Christians and Muslims on their boards, and some 400,000 Christians, including many Maronites, lived outside the entity's borders. Nevertheless, whatever Lebanon's future is to be, it would not be easy to pursuade the ultras to abandon what their enemies have called their "isolationism" and what they themselves have considered to be their integrity, even if the price be the abandonment of Greater Lebanon in favor of partition. In 1982, however, their strategy has been to attempt to reconstitute Lebanon, as much as possible, in their own image. The expulsion of the armed PLO by Israel, and Kata'ib success in winning the presidency for Bashir Gemayel and, after the latter's assassination, for Amin Gemayel, has provided the Kata'ib with this near-miraculous opportunity.

During the 1976–1982 interlude, in spite of all their suffering and difficulties, the Lebanese continued to exhibit their remarkable entre-preneurial vitality. Tradesmen in Beirut whose shops or even streets were devastated during the Civil War moved to open sidewalks to continue business; "service" (group taxi) stations quickly relocated to less dangerous spots; and enterprises such as Middle East Airlines continued in operation. The old saw about the Lebanese child who, asked what four and five make, answers, "Are you buying or selling?" was still pertinent. After the Israeli invasion this entrepreneurial vitality was shown in the resumption of regular services of Middle East Airlines after the airport opened on September 30, and faith in this vitality by Rafiq al-Hariri, a Sidon millionaire, who contributed several million dollars and his own heavy equipment to clean up west Beirut.

The quality of life in Lebanon, in general, however, continued to be dismal. And innumerable minor and intramural battles, in some cases involving little more than protection gangs fighting over turf, continued to be a common feature. In August 1981, for example, U.S. journalist John Kifner, whose count of private armies was fifty-four, of deaths for the month about 100, noted the following current confron-tations:[4] Lebanese leftists and Palestinians had clashed with Syrians; Shi'ites of al-Amal had clashed with Communists; Maronites had clashed

Reconstructing Beirut in the early 1980s. (Credit: *Middle East Insight*)

with one another; and a new unit of Syrians, consisting apparently of members of the special military force of Rifaat Asad, the Syrian president's brother, had taken up positions in west Beirut to challenge the Druze PSP forces of Walid Joumblatt, Kamal's son and heir as leftist leader. On August 22–23, east Beirut was pounded with artillery, suggesting to Kifner that "Lebanon was returning to normal." Except, he might have added, that because the July truce between the PLO and Israel was still in effect, there were for the moment no Phantoms screaming over the coast. In December the same correspondent, in a heart-rending description of Beirut indicated that two-thirds of the population were armed, the police often stuck to their sandbag-protected posts and provided little public order, and that of 300,000 subscribers to electricity, only 35,000 paid their bills regularly. Kifner quoted Samir Khalaf as saying that one was witnessing "the breakdown of a society."[5]

It would be as tedious as it is disheartening to detail the evidence for such pessimism. In months prior to the Israeli invasion, disasters that the Arab Follow-Up Committee (established to moderate between conflicting groups and composed of the Lebanese president, the secretary-general of the Arab League, and the foreign ministers of Lebanon, Syria, Kuwait, and Saudi Arabia) could do little to prevent included the following: explosions of booby-trapped cars, killing 83 and wounding 225 in early October and killing 7 and wounding 80 in February 1981— the little-known Organization for the Liberation of Lebanon from Foreigners claimed credit; assassinations, including those of Tahsin Atrash, a pro-Iraqi Ba'th leader, Abdel-Wahab Kayyali, once a member of the Executive Committee of the PLO, and the French ambassador, Louis Delamare, in the last months of 1981; the bombing of the Iraqi embassy by a suicide terrorist in December 1981, the same month violent fighting took place in Tripoli and the Akkar; and almost daily kidnappings and threats to life. In despair, Beirut's *L'Orient–Le Jour* on February 23, 1982, headlined the day's tragic events "La liste noire s'allonge" (the black list grows).

In April Palestinians and their leftist allies clashed with Shi'ites in south Beirut, and a minor French official and his wife were killed in cold blood. In May some fifty people were killed in clashes in Tripoli between the pro-Syrian Arab Democratic party and the Popular Resistance Movement; twelve died when a booby-trapped car exploded in the compound of the French Embassy. In west Beirut, in an attempt to establish "neighborhood councils" to provide the area with some order, the left was blocked by traditionalist Muslim leaders, and during the turbulence a Sunnite sheik was assassinated in Beirut, a Maronite priest in Aley. These were only some of the more egregious incidents of the day.

Looking at Lebanon in retrospect in June 1982, David Ignatius wrote: "It is clear something had to give in Lebanon. Syrian-controlled West Beirut had become, in the last few years, a city where the most basic rules of civilized behavior were suspended. Pedestrians worried more about car bombs than traffic. Embassy staff members were kidnapped and murdered. . . . Businessmen grew accustomed to paying off the various armed militias. The city was filled with the stench of garbage burning on vacant lots because nobody would collect it."[6] Lebanon had, in fact, become little more than an arena in which various international forces played out their rivalries, and a possible object of Syrian and Israeli irredentism and covetousness.

The most important rivalry was between Arabs and Israelis, of course, but more immediately it was the struggle between Palestinians and Israelis that had already led to so many interventions, to so much bloodshed, and to thousands of refugees inside Lebanon.

A second important rivalry played out on Lebanese soil was that between Syria and Egypt, who alternatively, for example, supported the Kata'ib and the PLO against the other. Since its entanglement with Israel and its forfeiture, temporarily, of leadership in the Arab world, Egypt has resented and been dismayed at Syria's leading role in Lebanon and the support for this role by the United States; Syria's position has weakened Egypt's previous role as leading peacemaker in the region.

A third rivalry was that between Syria and the Palestinians, each needing the other and each suspicious of the other. Syria has hoped to bring the Palestinians under a common command and on occasion asked the Palestinians to recognize Palestine as the southern part of a Greater Syria of which Damascus would be the natural leader. The Palestinians, naturally, refused to submit themselves to the sort of control exercised over their compatriots in Syria or to subordinate their strategy against Israel to Syria's.

A fourth rivalry was that between Iraq and Syria, perennial rivals for leadership in the Fertile Crescent and as exponents of Ba'th ideology. Each supported different elements among the Palestinians, and because of the Iran-Iraq war, Syria benefited from Shi'ite opposition to the Iraqi presence in Lebanon, represented mainly by the pro-Iraqi branch of the Ba'th party.

A fifth rivalry was that between the USSR and the United States for influence in the area, with the USSR supporting the Palestinians and the left—but frequently being caught between the rivalries among its clients (Syria and Iraq, Syria and the Palestinians)—and the United States seeking to exclude the Soviet Union from the area but tied to the isolated Anwar Sadat and handicapped by the intransigence of Menachem Begin.

And in this labyrinth, of course, many others sought advantage, including Libya in support of the left, Saudi Arabia in support of the moderates and conservatives (at one time even aiding the Kata'ib financially), Tehran in support of the Shi'ites, and others in the wings.

Finally, Lebanon felt threatened by the perceived or real irredentism of its two neighbors. Israel is perceived to covet southern Lebanon for biblical reasons and to serve as a defensive buttress against Syria as well as an offensive launching pad in the event of war. And Syria had never recognized the justice of the creation of Greater Lebanon and, more generally, had considered Lebanon a part of Greater Syria and of the "Arab nation." Friction between the two had been a regular feature of their relations over the years, exacerbated by differing economic philosophies, the treatment meted out to the roughly 400,000 Syrian migrants who once worked in Lebanon, Lebanon's having served as a haven for overthrown Syrian leaders and outlawed parties, and hostile criticisms of Syria in Lebanon's free press. After 1976, Syria was frustrated by its apparent inability to weld the different pieces in Lebanon together or to bring either the Palestinians, morally supported by other Arab states, or the Lebanese Front, supported to date by Israel, under its control. Both sides were important to Syria, each to check the other. And as an Arab state yearning for regional leadership, Syria was obliged to continue to support the Palestinian cause, but without allowing this to become the tail that wags the dog.

PROPOSALS FOR RECONSTRUCTION

In spite of so much internal anarchy and so many conflicting pressures, the Lebanese political structure survived, and Lebanon's leaders continued to seek solutions to the country's seemingly intractable problems. Some of the solutions proposed, although not implemented at the time, could prove useful in the future.

In the spring of 1980 the Sarkis government drafted a fourteen-point proposal to serve as a basis for national reconstruction.[7] This document serves to pinpoint some of the problems that still need to be confronted, and it also serves as a summary statement of what has ailed the Lebanese polity, if only by implication—even if it is now obsolete. The following steps were proposed:

1. The reestablishment of Lebanese sovereignty (in collaboration with the Arab Deterrent Force) over all regions and institutions.
2. Adherence to the democratic system and "cultural openness to the civilization of the world."

A Beirut market after the Syrian occupation—a grinning Lebanese merchant, a Syrian soldier. (Credit: Donna Egan)

3. Adherence to "the free economic system," but with state regulation and comprehensive planning to reconstruct and to strengthen the economic and social infrastructure.

4. Emphasis upon social justice, and "the creation of the appropriate conditions to deal with the question of sectarianism in the future."

5. Assertion that Lebanon is an "Arab state," loyal to the Arab League Charter, coordinating its efforts with other Arab states against "the Zionist enemy" and "strengthening Arab ranks in the struggle for Arab nationalist causes."

6. Full cooperation with other Arab states, but "with mutual respect for the independence, sovereignty and system and laws of each state, and non-interference in each other's internal affairs."

7. Support for the Palestinian cause, and rejection of the Camp David accords "on the grounds that these do not constitute a sound framework for a just and durable peace in the region" and "do not guarantee the legitimate rights of the Palestinian people, including the right to statehood on its own Palestinian homeland, and could ultimately lead to the resettlement of the Palestinians within the countries that now host them."

8. Insistence on the full implementation of U.N. Security Council resolutions regarding the south "with a view to ending the Israeli occupation of the border strip and re-establishing the sovereignty of the state on all parts of the South without any exception up to the internationally recognized borders" (on the basis of the Armistice Agreement between Israel and Lebanon of March 23, 1949).

9. "Rejection of all forms of collaboration and cooperation with the Israeli enemy."

10. While recognizing special fraternal relations with Syria, and close cooperation with her, assurance of "mutual respect for the independence, sovereignty and system of each country."

11. Implementation of existing agreements with the PLO, and cooperation with it, but "soundly within the framework of Lebanon's safety and sovereignty."

12. Cooperation with other nations within the framework of the United Nations while rejecting "the policy of alignments."

13. Development of relations with Lebanese emigrants and consolidation of the role of the Lebanese World Cultural League to serve Lebanon and its causes.

14. Treatment of these principles "as an integrated and indivisible whole."

Some thorny questions were evaded in these proposals—the physical presence of the Palestinians, for example, and whether to assimilate
those who wished or were forced to remain in Lebanon (and so further
jeopardize the sectarian balance). To please both the National Movement
and the Lebanese Front, apparent contradictions were allowed to stand,
such as allegiance to both Lebanese sovereignty and Pan-Arab ideals.
Any serious consideration of the issue of sectarianism itself was to be
postponed. And not discussed, except by implication, was the nature
and structure of the Lebanese army. In the latter case, however, a law
was passed by Parliament in 1979 providing for a degree of overall
control over this institution that has been virtually a monopoly of
Maronite officers and of the commander in chief. A Higher Defense
Council (including the president, the prime minister, and the ministers
of foreign affairs, interior, defense, and finance) was to execute cabinet
decisions, and a Military Council of senior officers, chaired by the
minister of defense, was to supervise internal military arrangements.
This second council was to be sectarian, including a Maronite, a Sunnite,
a Shi'ite, a Greek Catholic, and a Greek Orthodox. The ultimate aim
was to recruit an army of 28,000 in eight divisions, 1,000 air force and
naval personnel, 6,000 trainees, and other elements, to constitute a total
of some 40,000. The defense budget in 1978 was LL 491 million.

It was clear that the army as a symbol of national sovereignty
was the only agency that might someday provide the government with
the means to reconstitute its authority. But for this to occur, the army
would need the equipment, confidence, and support it lacked and would
need to be recognized as truly representative of the Lebanese as a
whole. In 1982 it was estimated that 60 percent of the top officers and
55 percent of the lower officers were Christian. The majority of the
recruits were Muslim, as in 1976 when the army disintegrated—at that
time 65 percent of the officers were Christian. Many Muslims needed
to be persuaded that the army was not still Christian-dominated, many
Christians that the army would not become predominantly Muslim in
the future. Up to the 1982 Israeli invasion the reconstructed army
remained unable to assert itself adequately—in October 1981, for example, when it moved into 'Ayn al-Rummana, the Kata'ib was able to
force its evacuation without firing a shot, and this Beirut district was
finally returned to army control only when a pro-Kata'ibi army officer
was in command.

Pessimists could argue that Sarkis's fourteen points were no more
likely to form a basis for reconciliation than were another Fourteen
Points proposed in the past by another president, one with considerably
more clout. Pessimists, moreover, could point to much in the document
that was evasive and ambiguous. Were, for example, the Palestinians

who wished to remain in Lebanon, if disarmed, to be allowed to do so? One side would say certainly, the other would refuse to consider so dangerous a threat to the future balance in Lebanon. Was the president to continue to be a Maronite? Were the Christians in general, irrespective of what census figures might show, to continue to have the edge in power they needed to feel secure?

Optimists, on the other hand, might suggest that any solution would have to be based not only on compromise, but inevitably upon a degree of hypocrisy and evasiveness. Much would have to be left unwritten and much entrusted to time and to patience. Optimists could add that already the Constitutional Document proposed by President Franjiyya, providing for the president to be Maronite, for the prime minister to be elected by parliament rather than by the president, and for an equal distribution of seats in parliament had been widely accepted, if only by implication. As for the "unholy alliance" between the Kata'ib and Israel, a matter that might prevent any possible resolution of the issues, on the Christian side ultra leaders had already expressed doubts about it and eminent Greek Orthodox and Greek Catholic clergy had denounced it.

A basis for considerable consensus did exist, optimists would say, and one of them, Marius Deeb, suggested that hostility to the Syrian presence had become so universal among all sectors that a consensus on the part of most Lebanese might be in the making. The same could be said regarding the Palestinian presence. Perhaps, also, the tragedy the Lebanese had experienced in common would serve as an education in the perils of ideological rigidity and sectarian exclusiveness. One might fear that the opposite was happening; nevertheless there were indications that behind the scenes traditional leaders were negotiating with each other and that at least some confessional groupings, the Maronites and the Shi'ites, for example, now felt they had much to offer one another.

Whether the tentative efforts of the Sarkis government to resolve Lebanon's dilemmas should prove a useful contribution or not remained to be seen. For the time being, this phantom government could at least claim to have preserved the skeletal framework of a republic that most Lebanese still recognized as legitimate, while awaiting a realignment in the Middle Eastern kaleidoscope. In June 1982, this realignment came with a vengeance when the kaleidoscope was given a violent twist by the Israeli government.

NOTES

1. *Middle East*, April 1981, p. 54, based on figures of the U.N. High Commission for Refugees.

2. Henry Kamm, *New York Times*, June 17, 1982.
3. *Newsweek*, June 28, 1982.
4. *New York Times*, August 24, 1981.
5. *New York Times Magazine*, December 6, 1981.
6. *Wall Street Journal*, June 18, 1982.
7. *Middle East*, May 1980, p. 15.

8

The Israeli Invasion
and Its Sequels

By the spring of 1982, dark and ominous clouds lay over Lebanon, as Israeli leaders hinted at a possible invasion to attempt, presumably, to destroy the SAM-6's Syria had implanted in Lebanon, to crush the PLO (probably in alliance with the Lebanese ultras), and possibly to seize the headwaters of the Litani River. To counter this possibility, the United States exerted pressure in favor of maintaining the July 1981 cease-fire and sent Philip Habib back to the area to mediate in February 1982; the U.N. Security Council, in this same month, voted to increase the UNIFIL force by one thousand to help patrol the gap between its troops around Beaufort Castle. Some observers believed that only the soggy winter soil and pressure from the United States not to prejudice the final evacuation of the Sinai, which took place on April 25, had prevented Israel so far from invading. The Sinai was evacuated without a hitch, and as the ground hardened in spring, the moment was favorable for the Israelis to strike. The Arab world was sharply divided, with Egypt out of the running for the time being, Syria suffering from internal turmoil, Syria and Iraq at loggerheads, and Iraq involved in war with Iran; a world oil glut made the use of the oil weapon less probable; the USSR was involved with its own problems in Afghanistan and Poland; and a sympathetic president and secretary of state held power in the United States. Whether Israel, implicitly or explicitly, received the green light from the United States, as of course the USSR maintains, remains to be determined. But it is clear that while it was believed that Israel intended only to clear a 25-mile (40-kilometer) area north of its border—to bring "Peace to Galilee"—the U.S. government did seem to lend support and to see the invasion as a new "opportunity" to realize some sort of overall solution.

It was only after much of world opinion had been revolted by the heavy civilian casualties the Israeli sweep involved, and when it had become clear that Ariel Sharon's grand strategy was to completely crush the PLO that the United States began to impose pressure upon Israel to suspend the "final solution," the phrase with its gruesome echoes sometimes used at the time. The invasion showed that Israel had opted for a violent rather than a negotiated solution to the Palestinian problem, this evidently to further a design that was made blatantly clear in a map Sharon would show journalists and others, one depicting the West Bank as Israeli, Jordan as Palestinian, and Lebanon as Christian.[1] Andre Fontaine of Le Monde spoke of a new Pax Hebraica, Joseph Harsch of the Christian Science Monitor of "imperial Israel." It remained to be seen whether Israel had not underestimated the depth and extension of Palestinian nationalism and whether it had not opened the floodgates to a new wave of radicalism, terrorism, and Islamic revivalism, costly to moderate Arab regimes, the interests of the United States, and ultimately dangerous to Israel itself. Whatever history's judgment might be, however, for Lebanon this invasion meant unparalleled human and physical destruction; it threatened either to split this already schizophrenic people as never before or to provide the nation with a fresh opportunity to reestablish its integrity.

Harbingers of the invasion included intrusions into Lebanese territory by Israeli sea and land patrols in February and March. Claiming that the cease-fire arranged by Habib applied to any point in the world, Israel bombed Palestinian camps in Lebanon from the air and from the sea in response to what it held to be violations—the killing of an Israeli soldier in Gaza in March, the shooting of an Israeli diplomat in Paris, the killing of an Israeli soldier by a land-mine in Lebanese territory in April, and two bombings within Israel in May. In spite of provocation—the "retaliatory" Israeli air attacks and the growing oppression of the Arab population in Gaza and the West Bank—the PLO held its fire. Large Israeli troop movements to the border, meanwhile, made clear something was in the offing. On June 3 came the final pretext for Israel, when the Israeli ambassador to London was shot by members of a dissident Palestinian splinter group. Renewed shelling of Palestinian positions finally led to the PLO's shelling of Israel. This was interpreted by Israel as a definitive repudiation of the cease-fire, and on June 6 Israel struck.

The massive invasion that now began involved an Israeli army of some 80,000, with 500 tanks. Complete control of the air as well as the sea was rapidly established. Syria was eliminated as a military factor when on June 9 its air force was knocked out of the sky—more than seventy Syrian planes were destroyed, with no losses for Israel. On June 11, Syria was forced to agree to a cease-fire. The blitzkrieg moved relentlessly on to the outskirts of Beirut where, by the middle of the

Israeli soldiers relaxing in Ba'abda, southeast of Beirut. (Credit: *Middle East Insight*)

month, some 7,000 PLO combatants and the PLO command, as well as several thousand Syrian troops, were totally besieged in west Beirut. Opposition from the other Arab states was only rhetorical—Libya's Qaddhafi proposed that the PLO leadership commit symbolic suicide—and unlike its forceful reaction in 1973, the USSR seemed relatively passive, as if accepting the crisis as falling within the preserve of the United States.

But then the Israeli sweep was halted and mired in a complicated diplomatic morass. Already having lost more than 200 men, interpreted as a large number for so small a country, Israel hesitated to penetrate the heavily armed and determined city, and increasingly world opinion, including now the United States, urged a negotiated resolution. What ensued was a complicated and confusing series of indirectly delivered messages. "It is as if a dozen people sat down together to weave a carpet, but each had a different design in mind."² At the risk of oversimplification, one might summarize the issues as follows: Arafat, while willing to withdraw his forces from Beirut, insisted upon main-taining a token military and political presence (in part to protect the thousands of civilian Palestinians who would remain behind); Israel insisted on a complete military and political withdrawal. In an effort to win over world opinion, Arafat repeated his position that the PLO would recognize Israel should Israel agree to a two-nation solution and the right of the Palestinians to "self-determination." To this Israel turned a deaf ear. To compound the problem, Philip Habib, the chief U.S. negotiator, had to persuade other Arab countries to play host to the PLO combatants, a herculean task for two reasons: Other Arab states did not want a truculent Palestinian presence in their midst, and they did not wish to appear to collaborate in a solution favorable to Israel.

In spite of Israeli efforts to minimize the human cost of their invasion, to present their sweep as unusually humane, and to blur through censorship of television images the impact of the inevitable cruelty involved, it soon became clear to the world that the price was indeed high. Thousands of civilians had been killed, tens of thousands rendered homeless, and parts of west Beirut were being reduced through frequent bombing to something like Dresden or Berlin during World War II. Gaza hospital reported in June that 90 percent of the casualties it treated were civilians, 60 percent of these women and children; Barbir hospital on the Green Line in west Beirut reported that by mid-July 250 had died on arrival or after being admitted (Dr. Amal Shamma angrily denounced Israeli's reduced figures as "lies"); the hospital of the American University of Beirut treated some 1,000 casualties in June. "Our hospital," said one official of the university, "is functioning much like a MASH unit." The Beirut newspaper *Al-Nahar* estimated that since the invasion and the end of the siege of Beirut 17,825 people had been killed, 30,103 wounded in all of Lebanon.[3] According to the Israeli government, Israel had lost 340 dead and some 2,000 wounded.[4]

Initial Lebanese reactions, even among the Muslims, to the Israeli invasion were, on the whole, less unfavorable than one might have expected. Journalists reported that most Lebanese wanted the PLO to evacuate Lebanon and catalogued the grievances of many Lebanese who had lived under PLO authority and their disillusionment with the Palestinian cause.[5] Many Lebanese resented Arafat's comparison during the siege of Beirut of himself to Churchill, who had remained in London during the blitz, and the declaration of some Palestinians that west Beirut would be their Stalingrad. Such Lebanese pointed out that Beirut was a Lebanese, not a Palestinian, city, and they saw little reason why it should remain hostage to an alien cause. One might remember, however, that the Syrians also had once been welcomed as deliverers.

One might generalize about the situation as follows, based on reports by journalists and other eyewitnesses. Most Christians, especially Maronites, were delighted by the Israeli sweep, and Israeli soldiers were welcomed into their towns with flowers. Israeli's invasion in July 1982 was of course a boon to the Kata'ib, but, paradoxically, it was also something of an embarrassment. Although it gave the ultras the op-

portunity to assume a dominating military role in Lebanon, they feared it might handicap Bashir Gemayel in his efforts to win the presidency by alienating the needed votes of Muslim deputies. One assumed it was for this reason that, while the Kata'ib helped to block west Beirut and to patrol towns and villages captured by the Israeli army, it did not engage in direct action against the PLO, letting the Israelis, so to speak, do the dirty work. And Gemayel made a point in July, to placate Muslim opinion, of traveling to Saudi Arabia and consulting with Walid Joumblatt.

The Kata'ib, of course, was not Israel's only Lebanese client or ally; there was also Major Haddad with his enclave in the south. With the invasion his sphere of control was extended north under the aegis of the Israelis—when Begin visited Beaufort Castle, Haddad was told it was now his! In some places, Sidon, for example, there was confrontation between officials representing the Kata'ib and the Haddad forces. One contrast between the two groups was that Haddad relied heavily on Shi'ite manpower—more than 60 percent of his 2,000-to-3,000-man armed force came from this community; claiming to represent them, he closed al-Amal offices in Nabatiyya and elsewhere as redundant. Begin made it clear that Haddad had his full support, and it appeared at the time that he would be the agent for Israel's satellization of southern Lebanon.

Shi'ites in the south, in general, appeared to welcome the Israeli invasion, happy to be free from Palestinian domination and from Israeli retaliatory raids. Elements of al-Amal in the north, however, in spite of tension between them and the PLO in the recent past, fought by the side of the PLO. The Druze reaction was also mixed. Majid Arslan, leader of the conservative wing of the Druzes, welcomed the invasion, and Walid Joumblatt, leader of the Lebanese leftists, in an extraordinary press interview on June 24, appeared to throw up his hands and declare both the PLO as a military force and his own Lebanese left as moribund. Druzes, however, resented the implantation in their towns by the Israelis of armed Kata'ib administrators, a factor that could easily militate against their sponsors.

Sunnite reaction was less easy to determine, but there were tensions between President Sarkis and the Sunnite prime minister, Shafiq al-Wazzan, and the traditionalist Sunnite leader Sa'b Salam in west Beirut played a salient role in the negotiations between Philip Habib and the PLO.

The phantom Lebanese government, meanwhile, responded to the invasion by appointing a Council of National Salvation to determine Lebanon's destiny. It included the prime minister, the foreign minister (Fuad Butros), Bashir Gemayel, Nabih Berri (head of al-Amal), Walid

Joumblatt, and the Greek Catholic deputy Nasri Maalouf. But much more would be needed to effect the "salvation" of Lebanon, and for the moment at least, crucial decisions were hardly likely to be made by the Lebanese themselves.

As the summer unfolded, the Israelis continued the siege of west Beirut, employing tactics that shocked world opinion. Food supplies, water, and electricity were cut off, and civilian as well as military targets were remorselessly shelled from land, sea, and air. By the beginning of August, however, it had become apparent that the occupation of the city would be unacceptably costly to all concerned—on August 4 the Israelis lost nineteen soldiers, with many more wounded in a thrust into peripheral areas, and on August 11, after the heaviest bombing by Israel to date, the U.S. government finally exerted unequivocal pressure upon the Begin government to allow Philip Habib to pursue his negotiations toward a peaceful evacuation of the city by the PLO.

By the end of August, there had been two important developments, but what these developments portended remained uncertain. The first was the implementation of the Habib plan and the actual withdrawal of the PLO and its Syrian allies from west Beirut and their relocation in other parts of the Arab world. The second was the election on August 23 of Bashir Gemayel as the new president of Lebanon.

The end of the PLO armed presence in west Beirut—even if PLO pockets remained in the south to continue to harass the Israelis and many hundreds remained in the north and in the Biqa' under the umbrella of the Syrian army—constituted a new act in the tragic drama of the Palestinian people. For the Lebanese ultras it represented a considerable victory; for the leftists and for many Muslims it meant that they had now lost their most powerful ally and were rendered militarily naked in face of the ultras and the Israelis. And for many Lebanese, both Christian and Muslim, it meant that there was now a prospect of a return to normal life after years of chaos and violence, however unpalatable the price to be paid and however well they might know that the Palestinian question would continue to haunt the Arab world and so themselves.

The second development, the election of Bashir Gemayel as president of Lebanon, was highly problematical. Gemayel was elected on the second ballot by fifty-seven votes out of a bare quorum of sixty-two (there were five blank votes) in the military barracks within Israeli-controlled territory in Beirut, with the aid of a minority of Muslim and Druze votes; there remained a question whether his election would receive national legitimization. Technically the election was legal and constitutional, but as many of the Kata'ib leader's opponents were quick to insist, it had taken place under the protection of the Israeli enemy

and with the use of tactics of bribery and intimidation by the Kata'ib. Before the election Muslim leaders meeting at the home of Sa'b Salam had called for a boycott of the election, and after the election they issued a statement that, although it did not exclude accepting the verdict, did refer to the election's "factional, dictatorial and fascist features" and described the election as having taken place while the "national public will was crippled by the Israeli military occupation." Rashid Karami, the veteran Sunnite leader, denounced the election; Walid Joumblatt stated, "Lebanon has now entered a huge prison"; and homes and businesses of a number of deputies who had voted for Gemayel were blown up.

The danger was, of course, that should Gemayel's election not be accepted by a major sector of the nation, the whole Lebanese system would be thrown into jeopardy, threatening to split the nation, once again, along the lines of the Civil War of 1975. The challenge now was whether Gemayel could transform his image from that of warlord and, to his enemies, "fascist," "terrorist," and "collaborator" with Israel, to that of national statesman. The Israelis were not helping by allowing the Kata'ib to establish its aegis over towns and villages that were not Maronite and by having Begin so effusively congratulate the new president-elect as "my dear friend" or by insisting upon a peace treaty with Lebanon. Such a treaty could threaten to exclude Lebanon from the Arab hinterland and its most important commercial markets, and, intolerable to most Muslims, cut Lebanon off from the rest of the Arab world. The Syrians made clear that official peace between Lebanon and Israel would mean war with Syria.

Bashir Gemayel's death in the explosion at the headquarters of the Kata'ib party in Beirut on September 14 ended, for the time being, both the Kata'ib and the Israeli strategies for Lebanon's future. This assassination was, as President Reagan expressed it, a "heinous crime," as well as a disaster, to most Maronites and also to all those of all sects who were prepared for a more tranquil dispensation, however authoritarian this might be. It was welcomed, on the other hand, by many Lebanese Muslims, Druzes, leftists, Palestinians, and by ex-president Franjiyya, among others. The prospect of Lebanon's transcending anarchy or finally ending civil war had suffered a serious setback.

By the end of summer, Syria remained a force in the north of Lebanon and in the Biqa'. Still to be resolved was the question of its presence in Lebanon. Two possibilities presented themselves regarding this presence. One, the Israelis would expel the Syrians by force and so totally dominate Lebanon, or two, weary of war and complying with world opinion, Israel would come to an implicit understanding with

Syria that the latter would, in effect, remain in the north and in the Biqa' and Israel would remain in the south. Should the second possibility eventuate, sovereign Lebanon would for all practical purposes be limited to Beirut and the Mountain. Whatever the outcome, it seemed probable that neither Syria nor Israel would leave Lebanon so long as the other remained there also.

Bashir Gemayel's declared intent had been to amalgamate armed militias, including his own Lebanese Forces, into an enlarged national army, to unite the nation, and to rid it of all foreign forces. But beholden to Israel, he had faced the dilemma of continuing to benefit from Israeli power and at the same time freeing himself from dependence upon Israel as it pressed for an immediate peace treaty. His assassination precipitated a fateful sequence of events. The Israeli army, in defiance of world opinion and their own agreements, seized west Beirut and then permitted Christian militiamen to enter the Palestinian camps of Sabra and Shatila, presumably to mop up remnants of the PLO. From September 15–18 (the dating is not yet clear) there followed the brutal massacre of hundreds of unarmed Palestinian civilians, to the horror of world opinion, including that of many Israelis. As if traumatized into temporary unity, on September 21 an unprecedented majority of deputies (77 of 80 present) elected Bashir's older brother, Amin, to be president on the first ballot.

Although lacking his brother's charisma or reputation for toughness, Amin, a politician rather than a warrior, was known to be conciliatory and less authoritarian than his brother and to have good relations with a number of Muslim leaders. In addition, he was less indebted than his brother to the Israelis. Dangerous, however, was a reported split within the Kata'ib between those who favored keeping their distance from Israel and those who favored a complete alliance with that country. It was alleged that this split was not unrelated to Bashir's assassination or to the last-minute effort to make Camille Chamoun a candidate for the presidency as a spoiler, an effort that proved abortive when Chamoun withdrew his name in the interests of national unity. Division within the Kata'ib was, of course, only one of a host of problems Amin now had to confront. Upon his inauguration on September 23, most of the nation over which he now presided was under the control of foreign armies with dubious commitments to Lebanon's national integrity.

Following Amin's inauguration, and through the fall of 1982, there prevailed a condition of stasis, with many minor confrontations but no major battle. But even as Beirutis celebrated the unification of their capital, and signs of the *dolce vita* reappeared in the western part of the city, the atmosphere there and in the country at large was hardly one of normality. In spite of the return after the Shatila-Sabra massacre of the French, Italian and U.S. multinational forces, which had previously been in Beirut briefly as part of the plan for the evacuation of the PLO, and the massive Israeli presence, clashes occurred between Kata'ib forces and Druze villagers; Israeli soldiers were occasionally attacked by roving bands; the Lebanese Army rounded up Palestinians in dragnet fashion and supervised the razing of illegal shanty houses, mostly occupied by Shi'ites; and evidence that the perpetrators of the Shatila-Sabra massacre had been top officers of the Kata'ib—even if this knowledge was muffled by many Lebanese, including Muslims, who wanted only to forget— served to poison the moral atmosphere. Nothing, in short, had been finally resolved, nor were the prospects propitious as the foreign armies on Lebanese soil prepared to bunker down for the coming winter and uprooted Palestinians sought improvised shelter as best they could. For the return to normality the Lebanese remained hostage to decisions to be made beyond their borders, in Jerusalem, Damascus, Riyadh, Amman, and Washington.

Given the multiplicity of variables involved in so complex a situation as the Lebanese, any predictions are impossible, except to say that it seemed in late 1982 almost certain that Lebanon, even if reconstituted in its integrity, would not be stable for months and most probably years ahead. No neat or conclusive ending to a book such as this seems possible, therefore, in the foreseeable future. The only recourse an author rash enough to publish now might have is to summarize, by way of a conclusion, three interrelated dilemmas Lebanon, should it regain its integrity, will have to live with and attempt to resolve.

First is the dilemma of identification, of developing a modicum of national consciousness (and conscience) together with loyalty to the nation, at the same time providing its various components with a sense of cultural and physical security. This will involve developing a sense of a common history, one that combines often disparate heritages, and transcending factionalism without sacrificing pluralism. This dilemma is compounded by the presence of about 400,000 Palestinians who, in spite of the military defeat of the PLO, are likely to remain a constant for a long time to come, if not permanently. Their integration will threaten to upset what sectarian balance still exists; their suppression can only involve further disruption.

Second is the dilemma of reestablishing conditions for the liberty, social, political, and economic, that the Lebanese have so prized and that has provided them with prosperity in the past, while overcoming anarchy. Government action must be taken to assure the poorer sectors of society and the underprivileged sects that they are not ignored, and government must assert its authority against license. To do this it will need a power base that is perceived as national rather than sectarian.

In the Lebanese context this would seem to be trying to square the circle.

The third dilemma involves Lebanon's stance on the international scene—how to sustain its freedom and security without jeopardizing its unity through alliances that threaten to smother and to polarize the nation internally. Israel for the ultras was such an ally in 1982.

Only an effective confrontation of these three dilemmas of identification, of liberty with social equity, and of autonomy with foreign assistance, will provide Lebanon with the opportunity of ceasing to be only an arena of international conflict and of becoming a genuinely sovereign republic. In the contemporary context the past can serve only to provide understanding; it can no longer provide a model. Lebanon must be restructured, not merely reconstituted.

NOTES

1. *Time,* June 14, 1982.
2. *New York Times,* July 8, 1982.
3. Ibid., September 2, 1982.
4. Ibid., September 6, 1982.
5. David Ignatius, *Wall Street Journal,* June 25, 1982; David Shipley, *New York Times,* July 25, 1982.

Selected and Annotated Bibliography

The intent of this bibliography is to provide the reader with pointers for further reading and information. It does not claim to be comprehensive. The references selected are principally but not exclusively in English; they are arranged roughly according to the succession of topics considered in the text.

SETTING, MULTIETHNICITY, IDENTIFICATIONS

Any general study of Lebanon will include a discussion of multiethnicity. Some useful sources, although they are now dated, are Pierre Rondot, *Les institutions politiques du Liban: Des communités traditionelles à l'état moderne* [Political institutions of Lebanon: From traditional communities to the modern state] (Paris: Imprimerie Nationale, 1947); and Albert Hourani, *Syria and Lebanon: A Political Essay* (London: Oxford University Press, 1946). More recent is Wilhelm Kewenig, *Die Koexistenz des Religios Gemeinschaften in Libanon* [The coexistence of religious communities in Lebanon] (Berlin: DeGruyter, 1965). For an analytical background and argument as to the transcendent importance of ethnic identification in Lebanon, see Samir Khalaf, *Persistence and Change in 19th Century Lebanon: A Sociological Essay* (Beirut: American University of Beirut, 1979). Khalaf is also the author of several articles on the subject, among them "The Americanization of the World: Western Perspectives on Modernization in Developing Societies," in *The Centrality of Science and Absolute Values* (International Cultural Foundation, 1975), pp. 1071–1095; and "Primordial Ties and Politics in Lebanon," *Middle Eastern Studies* 4 (April 1968):243–269. Also well worth consulting are articles by Paul Starr, particularly "Ethnic Categories and Identifications in Lebanon: A Descriptive Investigation," *Urban Life*, April 1978, pp. 111–142. A recent survey is Joseph Chamie, "Religious Groups in Lebanon: A Descriptive Investigation," *International Journal of Middle East Studies* 2 (1980):175–187.

For a radical disbelief in the Lebanese system from a Marxist point of view, see Halim Barakat, "Social and Political Integration in Lebanon: A Case of Social Mosaic," *Middle East Journal*, Summer 1973, pp. 301–318. For a more optimistic picture, see Iliya F. Harik, "The Ethnic Revolution and Political Integration in the Middle East," *International Journal of Middle East Affairs* 3, 3

(July 1972):303–323. Still helpful is Ralph Crow, "Religious Sectarianism in the Lebanese Political System," *Journal of Politics* 24 (August 1963):489–520. For a good up-to-date survey see W. B. Fisher, "Lebanon," in *The Middle East and North Africa 1979–80*, 26th ed. (London: Europa Publications, 1979), pp. 513–547.

HISTORY

A conventional treatment of Lebanon's history from prehistoric times to date of publication is Philip K. Hitti, *Lebanon in History* (London: Macmillan, 1957). Adel Ismail, *Histoire du Liban du XVIIe siècle a nos jours* [The history of Lebanon from the seventeenth century to our own time], Vols. I, II, IV (Paris: Maisonneuve, 1955–1958), covers the history of Lebanon for the years treated in the present text. An excellent, succinct, and readable political history is Kamal S. Salibi, *The Modern History of Lebanon* (London: Weidenfeld and Nicolson, 1965). To supplement this volume, see the lengthy review of it by Albert Hourani, "Lebanon from Feudalism to Modern State," *Middle Eastern Studies*, April 1966, pp. 256–263.

A fascinating travel account of Lebanon in the eighteenth century is Constantin-François Volney, *Travels Through Syria and Egypt in the Years 1783, 1784, and 1785*, 2 vols. (London: G.G.J. and J. Robinson, 1788).

First-rate monographs are Dominique Chevalier, *La société du Mont Liban à l'époque de la Révolution Industrielle en Europe* [The society of Mount Lebanon at the time of the Industrial Revolution in Europe] (Paris: Paul Guenther, 1971); William Polk, *The Opening of South Lebanon, 1788–1840* (Cambridge, Mass.: Harvard University Press, 1963); and Iliya F. Harik, *Politics and Change in a Traditional Society, Lebanon 1711–1845* (Princeton, N.J.: Princeton University Press, 1968). Also useful is Malcolm Kerr, *Lebanon in the Last Years of Feudalism, 1840–68: A Contemporary Account by Antūn Dāhir al-'Aqīqī and Other Documents* (Beirut: American University of Beirut, 1959). Eyewitness accounts well worth reading are Charles Churchill, *The Druzes and the Maronites Under Turkish Rule from 1840–1860* (London: Bernard Quairth, 1862); and Henry H. Jessup, *Fifty-Three Years in Syria* (New York: Fleming Revell Co., 1910).

There are a number of careful studies of the French mandate and the period preceding it. George Antonius, *The Arab Awakening* (London: Hamilton, 1938), is something of a classic even if it is now considered to exaggerate the extent of Arab nationalism before World War I. On this point see Zeine Zeine, *Arab-Turkish Relations and the Emergence of Arab Nationalism* (Beirut: Khayat's, 1958). Zeine argued that among the mass of Arab people, Arab nationalism began to replace loyalty to the Ottoman Empire only after 1908. Good monographs are John P. Spagnolo, *France and Ottoman Lebanon 1861–1914* (London: Ithaca Press, 1977); William I. Shorrock, *French Imperialism in the Middle East: The Failure of Policy in Syria and Lebanon* (Madison: University of Wisconsin Press, 1976); and Jan Karl Tanenbaum, *France and the Middle East: 1914–1920* (Philadelphia: American Philosophical Society, 1978). On the mandate period proper two solid studies are Albert Hourani, *Syria and Lebanon: A Political Essay* (London: Oxford University Press, 1946); and Stephen H. Longrigg, *Syria and Lebanon Under French Mandate* (London: Oxford University Press, 1958). An invaluable study of the thought and ideology of the period is Albert Hourani, *Arabic Thought in the Liberal Age 1798–1939* (London: Oxford University Press, 1962). See also A. L. Tibawi, *A Modern History of Greater Syria, Including Lebanon and Palestine* (London: Macmillan, 1969).

On Lebanon's more distant past and for those interested in tourism, see Nina Jidjian, *Byblos: Through the Ages* (Beirut: Dar el-Mashreq, 1968); *Beirut: Through the Ages* (Beirut: Dar El-Mashreq, 1973); and her other richly illustrated studies of Lebanese cities. Still useful is Bruce Condé, *See Lebanon: Over 100 Selected Trips with History and Pictures*, rev. ed. (Beirut: Harb Bijjani, 1960). A more recent guide is Philip Ward, *Touring Lebanon* (London: Faber and Faber, 1971). Handsome productions are George Taylor, *The Roman Temples of Lebanon: A Pictorial Guide* (Beirut: Dar el-Mashreq, 1967); and Friedrich Ragette, *Architecture in Lebanon: The Lebanese House During the 18th and 19th Centuries* (Beirut: American University of Beirut, 1974).

SOCIETY

Paul Starr, again, has done a great deal of fieldwork. See inter alia his "Social Patterns and Norms in Lebanon and the United States," *Human Relations* 29, 4 (1976):357–366. Offering fresh data as well as analysis are Edwin T. Prothro, *Child Rearing in the Lebanon*, Harvard Middle East Monograph Series no. 8 (Cambridge, Mass., 1961); and Prothro and Lutfy N. Diab, *Changing Family Patterns in the Arab East* (Beirut: American University of Beirut, 1974). A good study of class structure is Fuad L. Khuri, "The Changing Class Structure in Lebanon," *Middle East Journal*, Winter 1969, pp. 29–44. Among the large number of village studies are Judith R. Williams, *The Youth of Haouch el Harimi*, Harvard Middle East Monograph Series, no. 20 (Cambridge, Mass., 1968). A delightfully humorous account of an election is Elie Salem, "Local Elections in Lebanon: A Case Study," *Midwest Journal of Political Science* 9 (November 1965):376–387. A thorough study of a resort town is Richard Allouche, *Evolution d'un centre de villégiature au Liban (Broummana)* [Evolution of a summer resort in Lebanon (Broummana)] (Beirut: Dar el-Mashreq, 1970). Studies of cities include John Gulick, *Tripoli: A Muslim Arab City* (Cambridge, Mass.: Harvard University Press, 1967); Samir Khalaf and Per Kongstad, *Hamra of Beirut: A Case of Rapid Modernization* (London: E. J. Brill, 1973); and Fuad I. Khuri, *From Village to Suburbs: Order and Change in Greater Beirut* (Chicago: University of Chicago Press, 1975). Salwa C. Nassar Foundation for Lebanese Studies, *Beirut—Crossroads of Culture* (Beirut, 1970), contains some interesting essays, including Charles Malik's "Beirut—Crossroads of Culture," pp. 203–220. The data in Charles Churchill, *The City of Beirut: A Socio-Economic Survey* (Beirut: Dar al-Kitab, 1954) are still of at least historical interest, as are the data in David Yaukey, *Fertility Differences in a Modernizing Country* (Princeton, N.J.: Princeton University Press, 1961). More recent is Joseph Chamie, *Religion and Fertility* (Cambridge: Cambridge University Press, 1981). A good overall synthesis of studies of Lebanese society is Samih K. Farsoun, "Family Structure and Society in Modern Lebanon," in Louise E. Sweet, ed., *Peoples and Cultures of the Middle East: Volume II: Life in Cities, Towns and Countryside* (New York: Natural History Press, 1970), pp. 257–307.

An insightful impressionistic account of the Maronites is John Sykes, *The Mountain Arabs: A Window on the Middle East* (London: Hutchinson, 1968). Written from a special point of view but rich with material on Lebanese culture and literature, as well as much else, is Sélim Abou, *Le bilinguisme arabe-français au Liban* [Arab-French bilingualism in Lebanon] (Paris: Presses Universitaires de France, 1962). Abou's thesis is that Lebanon is as French as it is Arab, to its very core. A thorough and detailed study of Lebanese education and its social implications and ramifications is Theodor Hanf, *Erziehungswesen in Gesellschaft und Politik des Libanon* [Education in the society and polity of Lebanon] (Gütersloh: Bertelsmann, 1969). A recent history of the American University of Beirut is John Munro, *A Mutual Concern: The Story of the American University of Beirut* (Delmar, N.Y.: Caravan, 1977). On women's liberation, a path-breaker has been Leila Baalbaki's *Ana Ahya* [I live], translated by Michel Barbot as *Je vis!* (Paris: Seuil, 1958).

ECONOMY AND ADMINISTRATION

A basic source and a beginning point for any study of Lebanon's economy is *Besoins et possibilités du Liban: Etude préliminaire* [Needs and possibilities in Lebanon: Preliminary study], 2 vols. (Beirut: Lebanese Ministry of Planning, 1964), the survey by the French Institut International de Recherche et de Formation en vue du Développement (I.R.F.E.D.). Excellent monographs are Yusif Sayigh, *Entrepreneurs of Lebanon: The Role of the Business Leader in a Developing Economy* (Cambridge, Mass.: Harvard University Press, 1962); and Nadim Khalaf, *Economic Implications of the Size of Nations with Special Reference to Lebanon* (Leiden: Brill, 1971). Useful studies have been occasionally published by the Economic Research Institute at the American University of Beirut since its foundation in 1962. On economic and administrative reform, see George Grassmuck and Kamal Salibi, rev. ed., *Reformed Administration in Lebanon* (Beirut: Catholic Press, 1964); Adnan Iskandar, *Bureaucracy in Lebanon* (Beirut: American University of Beirut, 1964); and Abdo Baaklini, *Legislative and Political Development: Lebanon 1842–1972* (Durham, N.C.: Duke University Press, 1976). Making allowance for its unfortunate title, a useful synthesis is Elie Salem, *Modernization Without Revolution: Lebanon's Experience* (Bloomington: University of Indiana Press, 1973). Also a victim of faulty prophecy and timing, but with a great deal of useful data, is David and Audrey Smock, *The Politics of Pluralism: A Comparative Study of Lebanon and Ghana* (New York: Elsevier, 1975). Several works cited below also contain useful information on the economy and the administration of Lebanon.

POLITY

A starting point is *The Lebanese Constitution: A Reference* (Beirut: American University of Beirut, 1960). The most substantial study of Lebanon before 1975 is unquestionably Michael Hudson, *The Precarious Republic: Political Modernization in Lebanon* (New York: Random House, 1968), a work that has proved remarkably prophetic. More recent is Hudson's *Arab Politics: The Search for Legitimacy* (New Haven, Conn.: Yale University Press, 1977); Lebanon is discussed in pp. 280–296. Many important essays appear in Leonard Binder, ed., *Politics in Lebanon* (New York: John Wiley, 1966), in particular Malcolm Kerr, "Political Decision Making in a Confessional Democracy," pp. 187–212. Among the many studies of special usefulness are Michael Suleiman, *Political Parties in Lebanon: The Challenge of a Fragmented Political Culture* (Ithaca, N.Y.: Cornell University Press, 1967); John Entelis, *Pluralism and Party Transformation in Lebanon: al-Kata'ib 1936–1970* (Leiden: Brill, 1974); and Labib Zuwiyya-Yamak, *The Syrian Social Nationalist Party: An Ideological Analysis* (Cambridge, Mass.: Harvard University Press, 1966). For the rough sea in which Lebanon has had to navigate, see Malcolm

Kerr, *The Arab Cold War, Gamal 'Abd al-Nasir and His Rivals 1958–1970*, 3rd ed. (London: Oxford University Press, 1971). A good summary chapter is Joseph Malone, "Lebanon," in *The Arab Lands of Western Asia* (Englewood Cliffs, N.J.: Prentice-Hall, 1973), pp. 1–35. An interesting but partisan account of the civil troubles of 1958 is Camille Chamoun, *Crise au Moyen Orient* [Crisis in the Middle East] (Paris: Gallimard, 1963); an objective account is Fahim I. Qubain, *Crisis in Lebanon* (Washington, D.C.: Middle East Institute, 1961). For an intriguing, if not always discreet, personal account, see William Crane Eveland, *Ropes of Sand: America's Failure in the Middle East* (New York: W. W. Norton, 1980). Also personal in part is the author's own *Lebanon: The Fragmented Nation* (London: Croom Helm, 1980). An important article is Iliya F. Harik, "The Political Elite of Lebanon," in George Lenczowski, ed., *Political Elites in the Middle East* (Washington, D.C.: American Enterprise Institute for Public Policy Research, 1975), pp. 201–220.

THE CIVIL WAR AND AFTER

An analysis of the prelude to collapse, focusing upon student unrest in the first half of the 1970s, is Halim Barakat, *Lebanon in Strife: Student Preludes to the Civil War* (Austin: University of Texas Press, 1977). An interesting novel on student troubles on the eve of collapse is Tawfiq Yusuf Awwad, Leslie McLoughlin, trans., *Death in Beirut* (London: Heinemann, 1976).

Books on the background and the events of the Civil War are legion. First-rate on the early part of the Civil War is Kamal Salibi, *Crossroads to Civil War: Lebanon 1958–1976* (Delmar, N.Y.: Caravan, 1976). The best and most lucid analysis is probably Walid Khalidi, *Conflict and Violence in Lebanon: Confrontation in the Middle East* (Cambridge, Mass.: Harvard Center for International Affairs, 1979). Good also is Marius Deeb, *The Lebanese Civil War* (New York: Praeger Publishers, 1980). Two anthologies with essays of unequal merit are Roger Owen, ed., *Essays on the Crisis in Lebanon* (London: Ithaca Press, 1976); and P. Edward Haley and Lewis W. Snider, eds., *Lebanon in Crisis: Participants and Issues* (Syracuse, N.Y.: Syracuse University Press, 1979). In the latter volume particularly interesting are John Cooley, "The Palestinians," pp. 21–54, and Halim Barakat, "The Social Context," pp. 3–20. Other studies are John Bulloch, *Death of a Country* (London: Weidenfeld and Nicolson, 1977); René Chamussy, *Le Liban 1975–77* [Lebanon 1975–77] (Paris: Desclée, 1978); Thierry Desjardins, *Le martyre du Liban* [The martyrdom of Lebanon] (Paris: Plon, 1976); Pierre Vallaud, *Le Liban au bout du fusil* [Lebanon at the end of a gun] (Paris: Hachette, 1976); Albert Bourgi and Pierre Weiss, *Les complots libanais* [The Lebanese plots] (Paris: Berger-Levrault, 1978); and Ghassan Tueni, *Peace-Keeping Lebanon: The Facts, the Documents* (New York: William Belcher Group, 1980).

Of considerable interest is Kamal Joumblatt as collated by Philippe La- pousterle, *Pour le Liban* [In behalf of Lebanon] (Paris: Stock, 1978); in English, *I Speak for Lebanon* (London: Zed Press, 1982). Important articles include Michael Hudson, "The Lebanese Crisis: The Limits of Consociational Democracy," *Journal of Palestine Studies*, Spring-Summer 1976, pp. 109–122; Elizabeth Picard, "Rôle et évolution du Front Libanais dans la Guerre Civile" [The role and evolution of the Lebanese Front during the Civil War], *Maghreb-Machrek: Monde Arabe*, La Documentation Française, October-November-December 1980, pp. 16–39; Elie Salem, "Lebanon's Political Maze: The Search for Peace in a Troubled Land," *Middle East Journal*, Fall 1979, pp. 444–463; and his "Prospects for a

New Lebanon," *A.U.B. Newsletter*, Spring 1981, p. 608; Nadine Picaudou, "Les enjeux de la nouvelle crise libanaise: Partition 'de facto' et tentative de remodelage" [Stakes in Lebanon's new crisis: De facto partition and efforts to restructure], *Monde Diplomatique*, May 1981, p. 6; Selim Turquié, "De quoi vivent les libanais?" [How do the Lebanese live?], *Monde Diplomatique*, October 1979, pp. 1 and 6.

For a Marxist interpretation of the Civil War see Samih Farsoun and Walter Carroll, "The Civil War in Lebanon: Sect, Class and Imperialism," *Monthly Review: An Independent Socialist Magazine*, June 1976, pp. 12–37. A superb and very moving pamphlet is Jim Fine, *The Tragedy of Lebanon*, Middle East Peace Notes (Ann Arbor, Mich.: American Friends Service Committee, April 1981). Useful are Joseph Chamie, "The Lebanese Civil War: An Investigation into the Causes," *World Affairs* 139, 3 (Winter 1977):171–188, on the social background; and John P. Entelis, "The Politics of Partition: Christian Perspectives on Lebanon's Nationalist Identity," *International Insight*, May-June 1981, pp. 11–13. A discussion of the very popular radio program during the Civil War in which Jean Chamoun and Ziyad Rahbani commented upon the daily scene with acerbic satire is Janet Stevens, " 'We're Still O.K.'—The Lebanese Tapes," *Arab Studies Quarterly*, Autumn 1981, pp. 275–284.

A very useful survey analysis is Iliya Harik, *Lebanon: Anatomy of a Conflict*, American Universities Field Staff Reports, Asia Series, No. 49, 1981. Harik countered any Marxist interpretation of the Civil War and argued that the war was the result, in the main, of a political collapse produced by the Arab-Israeli conflict, distantly, and the Palestinian massive armed presence, immediately. Lebanon, he insisted, remains a viable model for multiethnic coexistence. For a Marxist, dependency-theory interpretation, see Salim Nasr, "Backdrop to Civil War: The Crisis of Lebanese Capitalism," *Middle East Research & Information Project* (MERIP) *Reports*, No. 73, (Washington, D.C., 1978), as well as Farsoun and Carroll, "The Civil War in Lebanon."

For evidence that Israel's intentions regarding Lebanon have been annexationist as well as defensive, see Livia Rokach, *Israel's Sacred Terrorism: A Study Based on Moshe Sharett's Personal Diary and Other Documents* (Belmont, Mass.: Association of Arab-American University Graduates, 1980). Early assessments of Lebanon's prospects in the summer of 1982 appear in the special issue of *Middle East Insight* 2, 4 (1982) entitled "Prospects for Peace in Lebanon."

NEWSPAPERS AND JOURNALS

It would be feckless to list all the papers and journals that touch upon the Middle East and provide current material. Among those this author has found particularly useful are *Le Monde*, the *Christian Science Monitor*, the *New York Times*, the *Manchester Guardian Weekly*, and Beirut's *L'Orient–Le Jour* (affiliate of the influential Arabic *Al-Nahar*). Interesting articles on Lebanon occasionally appear in the *Wall Street Journal*. Important articles on Lebanon often appear in the *Middle East* (London), the *Middle East Journal*, *Maghreb-Machrek*, *Le Monde Diplomatique*, and *Travaux et Jours* (Beirut). For domestic economic coverage see Beirut's *Le Commerce du Levant*. Of considerable importance as a documentary source on current affairs are the reports issued by the Modern Center for the Study of the Modern Arab World, the CEMAM reports (Beirut: Dar el-Mashreq for St. Joseph). An influential publication on economics is *Middle East Economic Survey* (Nicosia, Cyprus).

Index

116
Huntington, Samuel, 116
Hussein (king of Jordan), 29

Ibrahim, Muhsin, 88, 89
Ibrahim, Pasha, 17
Iddi, Emile, 22, 25(table), 86, 96
Iddi, Pierre, 86
Iddi, Raymond, 27, 86–87, 99, 130
Iddi family, 25
Idris, Suhail, 46
Ignatius, David, 134
Imam, 9
Independent Nasserist Movement,
    88
Industrial Census (1955), 34
Influence. *See Wasta*
Inheritance, 84
Institut d'Archéologie, 51
Interior, Ministry of, 84
International Airport (Beirut) (1951),
    59, 61, 72, 104, 108, 121(map)
International Bank, 71
Intra Bank, 65
Iran, 128. *See also* Lebanon, and
    Iran
Iranian revolution (1978–1979), 90,
    124, 129
Iran-Iraq war, 124, 129, 141
Iraq, 8, 27, 36(table), 49, 59(table),
    91, 117, 128
  nuclear plant, 124
  and Syria, 134, 141
  See also Ba'th parties; Lebanon,
    and Iraq;   Palestinians, and
    Iraq
Irredentism, 90, 134, 135
Islam, 14, 36, 115. *See also* Mus-
    lims
Israel (1948), 2, 3, 10, 26
  Druzes in, 10
  modernization, 36(table)
  and PLO, 104, 117, 122, 124,
    131, 133, 141, 142–144
  Security Belt, 120(map)
  See also Lebanon, and Israel;
    Lebanon, Israeli invasion; Ma-

ronite Phalangist party, and Is-
    rael; Palestinians, and Israel;
    Syria, and Israel; United States,
    and Israel
Italy, 59(table). *See also* Lebanon,
    and Italy
Iyad, Abu, 94

Jacobites (Syrian sect), 5
Ja'fari school of law. *See Sharia'*
Jam'iyyat al-Maqasid al-Khayriyya
    al-Islamiyya. *See* Muslim Soci-
    ety of Benevolent Intentions
Japan, 21. *See also* Lebanon, and
    Japan
Jews, 9, 45
Jihad, Abud, 94
Jinan, al- (magazine) (1870), 24
Jordan, 10, 36(table), 59(table), 88.
    See also Aqaba; Lebanon, and
    Jordan; Palestinians, in Jordan
Joumblatt, Hikmat, 97
Joumblatt, Kamal, 13, 27, 38, 68,
    70, 80, 85, 88–89, 91, 92, 94,
    95–96, 97–99, 100–102, 111,
    117, 124
  mother. *See* Nazira, Sitt
Joumblatt, Walid, 85, 99, 133, 145,
    146, 147
Joumblatt family, 25
Jounieh (Lebanon), 73, 111, 130
Jouplain, M. *See* Nujaym, Bulus
Jour, Le (Beirut newspaper), 28. *See
    also Orient-Le Jour, L'*
Judiciary Council, 84
Justice, Ministry of, 84

Kaddoumi, Farouk, 94
Kahalla, al- (Lebanon), 100
"Kalashnikov generation," 125
Karamah (Jordan), 92
Karami, Rashid, 27, 68, 71, 78, 80,
    85, 99, 100, 106, 108, 147
Karami family, 25
Karantina area (Beirut), 106, 127
Kaslik (Lebanon), 130

Marun (monk), 5
Marun, Yuhanna (patriarch), 5
Marxism, 101, 115
Marxist political parties, 88–89
Maslakh, al-, area (Beirut), 106
MEA. *See* Middle East Airlines
Mediterranean mentality, 45
Mediterranean Sea, 2
Melchites. *See* Greek Catholics
Meouchy, Boulos, 27
Messianic savior. *See Mahdi*
Metempsychosis, 10
Middle East Airlines (MEA), 41,
    58–59, 104, 131
Military Council, 138
Militias, 77, 79, 86, 88, 89, 92, 93,
    99, 105(table), 124, 130, 131
Millet system, 19, 82
Mitawalis. *See* Shi'ites
*Modernization Without Revolution:
    Lebanon's Experience* (Salem),
    116
Monday Morning (Beirut newspa-
    per), 110
Monde, Le (Paris newspaper), 130,
    142
Monothelite, 5
Montagne inspirée, La (Corm), 46
Moslem Lebanon Today, 14
Mountain, 2, 4, 17, 19, 46, 66, 86,
    100, 107, 124, 130
Mousayliha castle, 3
Movement of the Disinherited, 128
    militia. *See* Amal, al-
Mubarak, Butrus, 23
Mubarak, Ignatius, 14, 129
Muhafazes. See Provincial governors
Muhammad, 9
Muhammad 'Ali (pasha of Egypt),
    17, 18, 38
Multinational forces, 149
Muslims, 4, 12–14, 19, 20, 21, 27,
    29, 35, 101, 112, 127, 147
    and business, 58, 66, 131
    education, 23, 24, 49, 50, 54, 78
    employment, 73

in government, 68, 71, 81, 83,
    107, 108
massacre (1975), 111
moderate, 104
political party. *See* Najjadah party
See also Druzes; Shi'ites; Sunnites
Muslim Society of Benevolent In-
    tentions (1878), 23
Mutassarifiate (1861–1864), 18,
    34(map)
Muwahiddun, 10

Nabatiyya (Lebanon), 125, 145
Naccache, George, 48, 98
Nahar, Al- (Beirut newspaper), 43,
    48, 144
Nahariya (Israel), 122
Nahda. See Arab Awakening
Nahj al-shihabi. See Shihabism
Nahr Ibrahim (river), 3
Nahr al-Kalb. *See* Dog River
Najjadah party, 85, 86(table)
Namur (militia), 99
Napoleon I (emperor of the
    French), 17, 18
Napoleon III (emperor of the
    French), 3
Nasser, Gamal Abdel, 11, 26, 50,
    88, 93, 99
Nasserism, 88, 97, 105, 106
Nasserist Organization–Corrective
    Movement, 88
National Assembly. *See* Lebanon,
    parliament
National Bloc party, 86, 130
National Command (Ba'th party),
    89
National Establishment for Invest-
    ment Insurance, 63
National Front, 88, 105(table), 107
National Institute of Public Admin-
    istration, 69, 83
National Liberal party (NLP), 71,
    86, 99, 105(table), 106, 130
    militia, 124
National Litani Authority (1954),
    68–69, 71